Battle Orders • 20

Rommel's Afrika Korps

Tobruk to El Alamein

Pier Paolo Battistelli

Consultant editor Dr Duncan Anderson • *Series editors* Marcus Cowper and Nikolai Bogdanovic

First published in 2006 by Osprey Publishing
Midland House, West Way, Botley, Oxford OX2 0PH, UK
443 Park Avenue South, New York, NY 10016, USA
E-mail: info@ospreypublishing.com

ISBN13: 978 1 84176 901 1

Editorial by Ilios Publishing, Oxford, UK (www.iliospublishing.com)
Cartography: Bounford.com, Huntingdon, UK
Page layouts: Bounford.com, Huntingdon, UK
Index by Glyn Sutcliffe
Originated by United Graphics Pte Ltd., Singapore
Printed in China through Bookbuilders
Typeset in Monotype Gill Sans and ITC Stone Serif
08 09 10 11 12   11 10 9 8 7 6 5 4 3 2
A CIP catalogue record for this book is available from the British Library.

FOR A CATALOGUE OF ALL BOOKS PUBLISHED BY OSPREY MILITARY AND
AVIATION PLEASE CONTACT:

NORTH AMERICA
Osprey Direct, C/O Random House Distribution Center, 400 Hahn Road, Westminster,
MD 21157, USA
E-mail: info@ospreydirect.com

ALL OTHER REGIONS
Osprey Direct UK, P.O. Box 140, Wellingborough, Northants, NN8 2FA, UK
E-mail: info@ospreydirect.co.uk

Acknowledgements

Although the name 'Afrika Korps' specifically designated one
particular corps in the German Army, it has often been applied
to all the German units in North Africa. For reasons of space this
title does not cover all the German units in the Western Desert,
neither it takes into account the Italian units that, on some
occasions, were part of the Afrika Korps. Instead it focuses on
the German divisions that fought between Tobruk and El Alamein
in 1941/42.

The author wishes to thank those who helped him in this
work: Antonio Attarantato, dottor (MA) Piero Crociani (Rome
University La Sapienza), Tenente Colonnello Antonio Di Gangi
(Ufficio Storico SME), dottor (MA) Alessandro Gionfrida (Ufficio
Storico SME), dottor (MA) Alberto Manca, dottor (MA) Andrea
Molinari, Carlo Pecchi, dottor (MA) Federico Peyrani, dottor
(MA) Angelo Luigi Pirocchi, Maresciallo Maurizio Saporiti (Ufficio
Storico SME), Dr. Thomas Schlemmer (IfZG München), Mr
Stephen Walton (IWM Department of Documents). Very special
thanks go to Tenente Colonnello Filippo Cappellano (Ufficio
Storico SME), whose assistance in research proved invaluable; to
Marcus Cowper, who answered my many questions with extreme
patience; to Roberto Machella (chairman of the Military Historical
Center), whose work with microfilms is beyond any thanks; to
Dr Christopher Pugsley (RMA Sandhurst) and Dr Klaus Schmider
(RMA Sandhurst), who kindly revised the text. Any omission or
mistake is entirely my own.

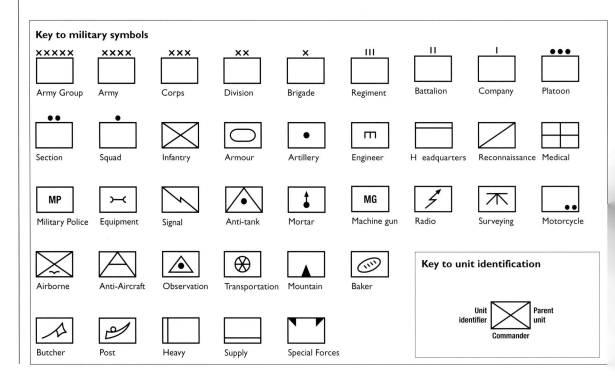

Key to military symbols

Army Group	Army	Corps	Division	Brigade	Regiment	Battalion	Company	Platoon
Section	Squad	Infantry	Armour	Artillery	Engineer	Headquarters	Reconnaissance	Medical
Military Police	Equipment	Signal	Anti-tank	Mortar	Machine gun	Radio	Surveying	Motorcycle
Airborne	Anti-Aircraft	Observation	Transportation	Mountain	Baker			
Butcher	Post	Heavy	Supply	Special Forces				

Key to unit identification

Unit identifier · Parent unit · Commander

Contents

Introduction

On 11 February 1941 when the first German troops arrived in Libya, few would have predicted that the struggle for North Africa was just beginning. These German troops had been sent to help the Italians after their defeat at the hands of the British following Lt. Gen. Richard O'Connor's Operation *Compass*, which culminated in the destruction of an entire Italian army at the battle of Beda Fomm. Yet, against all the odds, two months later the vanguards of the Deutsches Afrika Korps (DAK), still under strength and led by an anonymous general, swept through Cyrenaica as far as the Egyptian border. For the next 18 months the DAK, along with Italian units grouped under Rommel's Panzergruppe/Panzerarmee Afrika, fought against British and Commonwealth troops for the control of the Western Desert. The DAK was beaten once, yet it was soon back on the offensive and eventually threatened to reach its goal: the Nile. At the end, however, it was defeated and withdrew back to Tunisia, where it fought its last stand.

During those 18 months of struggle, the DAK earned a well-deserved reputation as a first-class, elite fighting unit and its commander, Generalfeldmarschall Erwin Rommel, developed a reputation as a military genius. Such a reputation, however, was acquired the hard way: in a very short period of time German commanders and their troops had to learn how to fight a war in the desert – dealing with their enemies as well as the awful climate and terrain. Although the process was arduous, the results were impressive and that is the major reason that the DAK became the first example of a fully motorized force that successfully conducted mobile warfare against stronger enemy forces in harsh terrain. The other reason was Rommel, whose skills and capabilities turned him into a legend as a military commander.

The arrival. A mixed group of German and Italian soldiers watches a PzKpfw II Ausf. C being disembarked at Tripoli harbour. Note how both the *Panzermänner* and other German soldiers are still wearing their European uniforms. Visible on the front hull of the PzKpfw II is the insignia of 3.Panzer Division. (Carlo Pecchi Collection)

4

Combat mission

The DAK was far from being an elite unit in early 1941. Though fully motorized, both divisions sent to North Africa had many drawbacks. The first unit sent, 5.leichte Division, was a hotchpotch of different units designed to serve in a defensive role. The unit that followed, 15.Panzer Division, was an armoured division at nearly full strength, but had only recently been transformed from an infantry division and lacked any real experience of armoured warfare. These drawbacks did not overly concern the German Army High Command, the Oberkommando des Heeres (OKH), as it only sought to fight a delaying action in North Africa until the conclusion of Operation *Barbarossa* – the invasion of the Soviet Union. A limited attack aimed at regaining Cyrenaica was authorized, but only after 15.Panzer Division arrived and the German troops had been properly trained and acclimatized. A major assault against Egypt was not envisaged until after the war against the Soviet Union had been brought to a satisfactory conclusion, probably by the end of 1941.

Rommel's bold sweep across Cyrenaica thwarted these plans, but the OKH could not adjust to the new reality as the Eastern Front was in desperate need of motor transport in general and mechanized troops in particular. Thus, in summer 1941 the DAK was stuck in a stalemate and, unsurprisingly, allowed the bare number of reinforcements by the OKH. The situation did not change much in 1942 despite Rommel's second drive into Cyrenaica, as both Hitler and the OKH were still gravely concerned about the difficult situation on the Eastern Front. As a consequence the Mediterranean remained a sideshow, although there was an overall strategic plan. This involved an assault aimed at the seizure of the port of Tobruk, which was to be followed by an invasion of Malta with the aim of bringing the supply problems to an end.

However, this plan did not take into account Rommel's new advance, this time into Egypt. Although there were no significant reinforcements available for the DAK, the OKH did try to improve the quality of its weaponry. For the

German lorries are disembarked at Tripoli harbour and, laden with the DAK's equipment and supplies, are ready to move to the front. Many German vehicles, like these Büssing-Nag 4 x 2 medium lorries shown here, were based on civilian models and proved unsuitable for the desert conditions. (Carlo Pecchi Collection)

German soldiers lined up somewhere in Libya, all wearing the DAK tropical uniform. Since two of them wear the 'Afrikakorps' cuff title, instituted on 18 July 1941, the photo can be dated to summer 1941. Tropical uniforms, actually unsuitable for the desert, were still largely used for ceremonies and formal occasions. (Archivio Ufficio Storico Stato Maggiore Esercito)

A DAK column moving across the streets of a Libyan town. The lorries, all sporting a neat 'palm with swastika' DAK insignia, appear to be still painted in the European dark-grey finish and only have a light coat of sand. The tactical insignia on the left mudguard is a divisional symbol. (Carlo Pecchi Collection)

first time the German Army sought to make good its shortcomings using improved weaponry and better balanced combat units – the 'fewer men, more weapons' solution. However, Rommel's unexpected successes at Gazala and Tobruk compelled Hitler to authorize a premature advance into Egypt. The result was that, by the end of July, for the first time a strained DAK faced a severe crisis and was in real danger of breaking down. As a consequence new reinforcements were brought in, although it was too little too late: having failed to break through the British defences at El Alamein, the DAK had no other choice but to stand on the defensive and wait for the enemy offensive to be unleashed.

Always under strength and plagued by a perennial lack of weapons, vehicles and supplies, the DAK was nevertheless in better shape than many other units of the German Army. In many cases its equipment included modern weapons that were not available in large quantities. Though lacking in numbers, in early 1941 its tank inventory did not include any of the obsolete Czech tanks that were used on a large scale against the Soviet Union. Also, in 1942 it was supplied with some of the most modern weapons available. All in all, the DAK often fielded more and better weapons, vehicles and equipment than many of the motorized units on the Eastern Front. Such an odd state of affairs was remarked on by the OKH which pointed out how DAK's allocation of motor transport was $1/10$th of that available for *Barbarossa*, while its actual strength was only $1/78$th of the force committed to the invasion of the Soviet Union. A remarkable point that clearly shows how the DAK, in spite of its many shortcomings, established itself as an effective fighting force and a perfect prototype for fully motorized units.

Preparation for war: doctrine and training

In 1941 the DAK lacked both a specific doctrine for desert warfare and proper training for the job in hand. However, despite these shortcomings the German Army had already developed the most advanced armoured warfare doctrine of the time. Its root lay in the concept of *Bewegungskrieg* (movement warfare), deemed the only possible way to deal with stronger enemies and to avoid static, attritional warfare. The best manner to implement *Bewegungskrieg* was through offensive actions, which were to follow specific guidelines leading to a decision on the battlefield through the *Vernichtungsschlacht* (the battle of annihilation). These guidelines included concentration of force, combined-arms warfare and use of air power, all to be combined together against a selected *Schwerpunkt* (decisive point of effort). As soon as a breakthrough had been obtained it had to be exploited using speed, flexibility and manoeuvre to break into the enemy rear areas, and eventually envelop and destroy his forces. Armoured units played a major role in the doctrine of movement warfare since they were the units most suited to producing and exploiting a breakthrough in enemy lines. The *Panzerkeil* (armoured wedge) became a decisive factor in the German *Keil und Kessel* doctrine, based on the principles of the 'wedge and cauldron' to obtain the destruction of enemy forces.

However, the most important aspect of the German doctrine was the lack of any specific formula or rule; the doctrine only supplied guidelines, and commanders had to evaluate the situation by taking into account both the conditions of the terrain and the deployment of enemy forces. Rommel took full advantage of this lack of specificity when in March–April 1941, contrary to OKH directives, he decided to advance deeply into Cyrenaica. Although the whole area was seized (with the notable exception of Tobruk) and heavy losses were inflicted on British and Commonwealth troops[1], the campaign was disappointing from a doctrinal point of view. There had been neither a *Schwerpunkt* nor a *Vernichtungsschlacht* and, above all, British forces were able to retreat to Tobruk, which proved too hard a nut to crack for the DAK. As a matter of fact, DAK's first offensive is more reminiscent of the German stormtroop tactics, based on infiltration and pursuit, developed in the last year of World War I, which Rommel had first-hand experience of. The result was a stalemate and the hated *Stellungskrieg* (static warfare), for which the DAK was completely unfit.

---

1 Hereafter, 'British' will refer to British, Commonwealth and Indian units.

Rommel, accompanied by Italian officers (the one seated to the right of the photo, appears to be General Roatta, Italian Army chief-of-staff), prepares to parade German units before they head to the front. Note how all the German officers but one are still wearing their European uniforms. (Filippo Cappellano)

As soon as they arrived at Tripoli in February–March 1941, 5.leichte Division's units paraded through the streets before marching to the front. This seems to have been one of Rommel's ingenious tricks, aimed at showing everybody (British intelligence included) the mighty power of the German forces. The Horch Kfz 16 medium staff car, followed by BMW combinations, belongs to Panzer Aufklärungs Abteilung 3 (see tactical sign on the left mudguard). (Carlo Pecchi Collection)

However, the campaign of 1941 in Cyrenaica supplied valuable experience for the forces involved and led to Rommel concluding that the Western Desert 'was the only theatre where the principles of motorized and tank warfare, as they had been taught theoretically before the war, could be applied to the full – and further developed'. Unlike Europe, here pedestrian infantry units were useless unless employed in static, prepared positions; mobile and armoured units, on the other hand, ruled the battlefield. Therefore, the *Panzerkeil* doctrine could not be implemented in the same manner as in France or on the Eastern Front, where the infantry were tasked with surrounding and destroying cut-off enemy forces. The open terrain of the Western Desert also made it harder to encircle enemy mobile and armoured formations, since they could break the ring by concentrating their weight against a given point. Enemy units could be successfully encircled and annihilated only when they were pedestrian (that is either infantry or mobile units short of fuel), badly led or already shaken and disintegrating.

Given the numerical superiority of the British forces, it is remarkable how the DAK actually achieved such stunning victories. These were largely the result of further doctrinal developments coupled with British operational mistakes. One of Rommel's first attempts to overcome the limitations of mobile warfare in the desert proved unsuccessful, although it also offered valuable experience. During Operation *Crusader*, on 24 November 1941, his 'dash to the wire' was a clear attempt to bring about the conditions that might have enabled the destruction of the enemy mobile forces. He sought this through an extension of the *Bewegungskrieg* doctrine – the penetration in depth. The aim was the destruction of British supply dumps and lines of communications,

BMW R75 combinations of Panzer Aufklärungs Abteilung 3 parading in Tripoli before marching due east, 15 February 1941. (Filippo Cappellano)

which, had it happened, would have brought about the paralysis – and subsequent destruction – of the British forces. Though not new, this doctrine was innovative when compared to the more 'conservative' one that simply envisaged encirclement and destruction of enemy forces by speed and manoeuvre. It had already been successfully tested in May–June 1940 on the Western Front, when the German penetration in depth paralysed French, British and Belgian forces (though some of them successfully escaped the trap by sea). However, in November 1941 it was a failure: Rommel had forgotten that mobile warfare also requires mobile supply dumps, which the British had actually placed away from the border and the DAK neither located nor destroyed.

An eight-wheeled Panzerfunkwagen SdKfz 263, a heavy communications armoured car mounting a 30-watt Funkgerät 8 with a large frame antenna. It probably belonged to 3.Kompanie/Nachrichten Abteilung 39 (mot). (Filippo Cappellano)

Given these premises it is not surprising that Rommel turned back to the concept of penetration in depth only once, and with a different approach, at El Alamein. In August 1942 his plan to attack the Alamein Line, which ended in the battle of Alam Halfa, was based on this concept. Once the *Panzerkeil* had broken the southernmost defences of the line, it was to move to the north-east until it reached the area south-west of El Hamman, some 40km east of Alamein and about 50km from the start line. Here, their flanks protected by infantry units, the armoured formations were to threaten the British supply areas thus compelling enemy motorized forces into a decisive battle in the open. The defeat of these forces should have brought about the collapse of the whole Alamein Line. Differences from the basic *Bewegungskrieg* doctrine are clearly noticeable: victory is not sought after the encirclement or paralysis of enemy forces, but rather through provoking an open battle in which Axis forces were superior to the British – at least in terms of tactical ability and manoeuvrability.

This is the approach Rommel took when he adapted the German *Bewegungskrieg* doctrine to warfare in the Western Desert. After the second drive into western Cyrenaica in January–February 1942 (which once again saw British units escaping the Axis' *Kessel*), Rommel decided to attack the British Gazala Line using classic *Flankenangriff* (flank attack) tactics. He intended to perform a turning movement (a 'hook') behind the British defences, which would then be attacked both frontally and from the rear. The encircled British infantry units would then be crushed and the Gazala Line destroyed. This

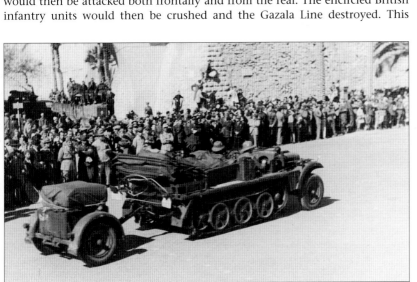

A 1-ton half-tracked Demag D7 SdKfz 10 with trailer on which the tactical insignia of a *Panzerjäger* unit is just visible. That makes it very likely part of the Panzerjäger Abteilung 39. (Carlo Pecchi Collection)

A brand-new looking 105mm leichte Feldhaubitze 18 towed by a 3-ton half-tracked Hanomag H kl 6 SdKfz 11 tractor in front of a large crowd of Italian and German officers. These quite clearly belong to 5.leichte Division's I.Abteilung/Artillerie Regiment 75. (Carlo Pecchi Collection)

would then provoke the British armoured and mobile forces into an open battle where the DAK could take full advantage of its better tactics, unit coordination, manoeuvrability and battlefield skill.

There are three specific points that are worth making about this plan. Firstly, fixed defences are only seen as a hindrance for the attacker, not as an overwhelming obstacle. Secondly, Rommel sought battle in the open, in which the DAK would have outmanoeuvred its adversaries, and thirdly he also sought to attain local superiority against an otherwise stronger enemy. Although the plan only lasted two days before the battle took a different course, the basic concepts of acquiring local superiority and of seeking battle in the open proved sound and successful. Subsequent developments of what remains Rommel's most successful campaign in the Western Desert followed the same pattern: British forces were surrounded in groups and, with the Germans taking advantage of local superiority, were destroyed piecemeal both at Tobruk and at Matruh.

The plan to attack the Alamein Line in July 1942 was not much different from the one that had been used at Gazala. British defences had to be broken close to El Alamein and then, while infantry formations protected the left

PzKpfw III Ausf. G (Trop) of I.Kompanie/Panzer Regiment 5 parading through the streets of Tripoli. Not only are they still painted in the dark-grey European scheme, but the crews are still wearing their black uniforms that would soon be replaced by tropical ones. (Carlo Pecchi Collection)

A column of PzKpfw II Ausf. Cs of Panzer Regiment 5, very likely belonging to one of II.Abteilung's *leichte Panzerzug*. The 1941 establishment of a Panzer regiment still included a large number of these light tanks. (Carlo Pecchi Collection)

wing, the *Panzerkeil* was to turn south and attack the British formations at the southernmost part of the line in the rear. Once more the concept was that of *Flankenangriff*, with the aim of achieving local superiority through manoeuvre rather than the encircling of a large body of troops. Unfortunately for Rommel and the DAK, the Axis forces were suffering from battle casualties and fatigue and in this particular instance the British actually achieved local superiority. Rommel's most successful campaign was over, just short of its goal.

It is worth noting that the doctrine Rommel implemented in the spring and summer of 1942 was not much different from the one Lt. Gen. Richard O'Connor used against the Italians between December 1940 and February 1941. The only difference was that in 1940–41 O'Connor faced largely non-motorized enemy formations still bound to doctrines and tactics inspired by 19th-century colonial warfare. This enabled him to deliver a fatal blow at Beda Fomm with a move very similar to those recommended by the German *Vernichtungsschlacht* doctrine. Rommel found it much harder against a largely motorized army whose doctrines and tactics, though very different from his own, were well suited to warfare in the Western Desert.

A *Panzerzug* of PzKpfw IIIs during what looks like a field-training session. Field training was given great emphasis as it enabled tank crews to gain an actual knowledge of the terrain and their vehicles. (Carlo Pecchi Collection)

Unit organization

Facing the Italian collapse in North Africa, on 9 January 1941 Hitler ordered the creation of a motorized blocking formation to be sent at once to Libya. Two days later, the OKH ordered the formation of Sperrverband Libyen, composed of Aufklärungs Abteilung 3, three *Panzerjäger Abteilungen* (39, 559 and 605, the latter with a *Panzer Kompanie* attached), two *Maschinengewehre Bataillone* (2 and 8) and I./Flak Abteilung 33 from the Luftwaffe. Generalleutnant Hans von Funck, commander of 3.Panzer Brigade (whose Stab became that of the division) was the commanding officer. On 14 January the unit was renamed leichte motorisierte Division Funck and, shortly thereafter, 5.leichte Division. On 3 February Hitler decided to replace von Funck with Generalleutnant Erwin Rommel and ordered an increase in the strength of the division. On 10 February, the OKH eventually ordered the reorganization of 5.leichte Division to include a full Panzer regiment, and created the Stab der Befehlshaber der deutschen Truppen in Libyen, Rommel's own command. On 18 February Hitler decided that an entire German corps was needed and ordered that a full Panzer division be sent as well. The following day orders were issued renaming Rommel's command as the Deutsches Afrika Korps – the German Corps for Africa.

The bulk of 5.leichte Division was supplied by 3.Panzer Division, which gave its Stab 3.Panzerbrigade (forming the divisional Stab), Panzer Regiment 5, Aufklärungs Abteilung 3, I./Artillerie Regiment 75, 2.Kompanie/Panzer Pionier Bataillon 39, 3./Panzer Nachrichten Abteilung 39, Panzerjäger Abteilung 39 and 1./Sanitäts Kompanie 83. Other units were corps troops (**Fig. 1**). This division had a unique organizational structure, unlike any other contemporary German unit and very different to the old *leichte Divisionen*, which were cavalry divisions with an attached *Panzer Abteilung* (they had been disbanded in late 1939 to form new Panzer divisions). 5.leichte Division was a tank and anti-tank heavy unit, with an established strength of about 90 medium and 70 light tanks, and about 150 anti-tank and anti-aircraft guns, of which more than 60 were self-propelled. This is quite remarkable considering its established strength of 12,000 men with only two infantry and one artillery battalions. The division arrived in Libya between 11 February and early April 1941, just in time to take part in Rommel's first drive into Cyrenaica. 15.Panzer Division, which had been chosen as the second German division to be sent to Africa on 26 February 1941, followed almost immediately.

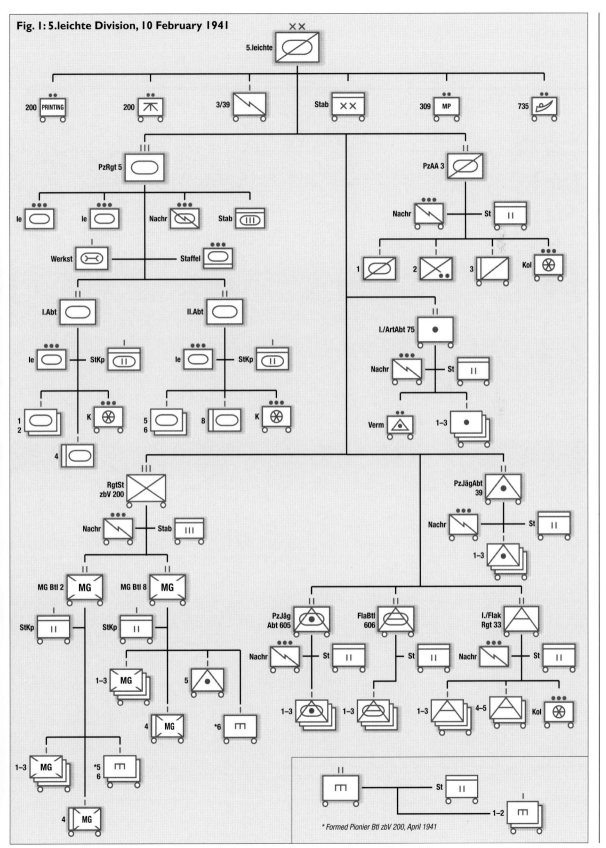

Fig. 1: 5.leichte Division, 10 February 1941

* Formed Pionier Btl zbV 200, April 1941

13

Table 1: 5.leichte Division, 10 February 1941

Generalmajor Johannes Streich from 13 February

Stab (mot)

3.Kp./Nachrichten Abt. 39 (mot)

Div.Kartenstelle 200 (mot)

Drückereitrupp 200 (mot)

Panzer Rgt. 5

Stab

Panzer Nachrichtenzug

leichte Panzerzug

leichte Panzerzug

Panzerwerkstatt Kompanie

Panzer Staffel

I.Abteilung

    Stabskompanie

    leichte Panzerzug

    1.–2.leichte Panzerkompanie

    4.mittlere Panzerkompanie

    leichte Panzerkolonne

II.Abteilung

    Stabskompanie

    leichte Panzerzug

    5.–6.leichte Panzerkompanie

    8.mittlere Panzerkompanie

    leichte Panzerkolonne

Regiments Stab zbV 200 (mot)

Stab (mot)

Nachrichtenzug (mot)

MG Bataillon 2 (mot)

    Stabskompanie (mot)

    1.–3.MG Schützen Kp. (mot)

    4.schwere Kompanie (mot)

    5.–6.(Pionier) Komp. (mot) *

MG Bataillon 8 (mot)

    Stabskompanie (mot)

    1.-3.MG Schützen Kp. (mot)

    4.schwere Kompanie (mot)

    5.Panzerjäger Kp. (mot)

    6.(Pionier) Komp. (mot) *

Pz.Aufklärungs Abt.3 (mot)

Stab (mot)

Nachrichtenzug (mot)

1.Panzerspäh Komp. (mot)

2.Kradschützen Kp. (mot)

3.schwere Kompanie (mot)

leichte Kolonne (mot)

I.Abt./Artillerie Rgt. 75 (mot)

Stab (mot)

Nachrichtenzug (mot)

Vermessungstrupp (mot)

1.–3.leichte Batterie (mot)

Panzerjäger Abt. 39 (mot)

Stab (mot)

Nachrichtenzug (mot)

1.–3.Panzerjäger Komp. (mot)

Panzerjäger Abt. 605 (sfl)

Stab (mot)

Nachrichtenzug (mot)

1.–3.Panzerjäger Komp. (sfl)

Fla Bataillon 606 (mot)

Stab (mot)

1.–3.Kompanie (sfl)

I.Abt./Flak Rgt. 33 (mot)

Stab (mot)

Nachrichtenzug (teilmot – partly motorized)

1.–3.schwere Flak Batterie (88mm) (mot)

4.–5.leichte Flak Batterie (20mm) (mot)

schwere Flak Kolonne (teilmot – partly motorized)

Feldgendarmerietrupp 309 (mot)

Feldpostamt zbV 735 (mot)

Divisions Verpflegungsamt 341 (mot)

Bäckerei Kompanie 531 (mot)

14   *(continues on page 15)*

Schlachterei Kompanie 503 (mot)	
Sanitäts Kompanie 1/83, 2/592 (mot)	
Feldlazarett 4/572 (mot)	
Krankenkraftwagenzug 631, 633 (mot)	
Filtergerät Kolonne 877 (mot)	

* 5./MG Btl. 2 from 2./Pz.Pion.Btl. 39, 6./MG Btl. 2 from 2./Pz.Pion.Btl. 33
5./MG Btl. 2 and 6./MG Btl. 8 formed Pionier Bataillon zbV 200, April 1941 (6./MG Btl.
2 returned to 15. Pz.Div.)

Notes
*At its arrival in Libya, 5.leichte Division had an array of supply, service and transportation
units including (amongst others):
Entladen Stab zbV 681, Verladen Stab zbV 683, Nachschub Abteilung 532, 533, 619 and
668 zbV (all motorized).
Of these, only the latter remained under divisional control, assuming the role of Divisions
Nachschub Führer (DiNaFü). In May 1941 it included:*
Nachschub Abteilung 668 zbV (mot)
*Kleine Kraftwagenkolonne 797, 800, 801, 803, 804, 822. Grosse Kraftwagenkolonne 5/619,
6/619, 622, 1 and 2/PzRgt 5 (detached). Nachschub Komp. 1/532, Werkstatt Komp. 1/532
(later 200). Panzer Ersatzteil Kolonne 1 (all motorized).*

This unit was formed on 1 November 1940 from 33.Infanterie Division and by mid-March 1941, when ordered to move, it was almost at full strength lacking only 2./Panzer Pionier Bataillon 33 (which had been used to form 6./MG Bataillon 2) and the bridging columns (**Fig. 2**). With an established strength of about 15,000 it was stronger in infantry and artillery than 5.leichte Division, but it only had about 50 anti-tank guns and 140 tanks, though its Panzer Regiments had a higher proportion of medium tanks (about 100). The division arrived in Africa between late March and mid-May 1941 and was deployed in the Sollum area. Some losses were suffered en route, including 11.(IG)/Schützen Regiment 115 and Panzer Nachrichten Abteilung 33, the latter eventually being replaced by Panzer Nachrichten Abteilung 78. Also, between early April and mid-May some changes occurred in the organization of 5.leichte Division. The MG Bataillon lost its Pionier Kompanie, 6./MG Bataillon 2 (which had been formed in mid-February from the 2./Panzer Pionier Bataillon 33 of 15. Panzer Division), which returned to its home unit, while 5./MG Bataillon 2 and 6./MG Bataillon 8 were used to form Pionier Bataillon zbV 200, whose Stab had been formed in Germany in early February and sent to Libya by mid/late April. By mid-May 1941 the composition of the DAK began to take shape, including (apart from the two divisions and supply troops) six infantry and four artillery battalions (two of the latter coastal), which were mainly used in security roles. Combat experience had already shown that neither this organization nor the total strength were appropriate for Rommel's planned offensive into Egypt.

On account of this, in late July 1941 the DAK requested from the OKH a major strengthening and reorganization of its divisions, plus the formation of a third motorized infantry division. These requests were a prerequisite for a successful Axis offensive into Egypt. The strength of each Panzer regiment needed to be increased so that each one had three four-company battalions (three light, one medium tanks). Increased supply and repair capacity, as well as an armoured supply column for use in hostile conditions, were also needed. Kradschützen Bataillon 15, having proved inadequate for the desert, was to be equipped with armoured personnel carriers. Also the strength of both *Panzer Aufklärungs Abteilungen* needed to be doubled to form reconnaissance regiments, as in their present form they were considered too weak for their role. Last but not least, more modern weapons – above all anti-tank and anti-aircraft

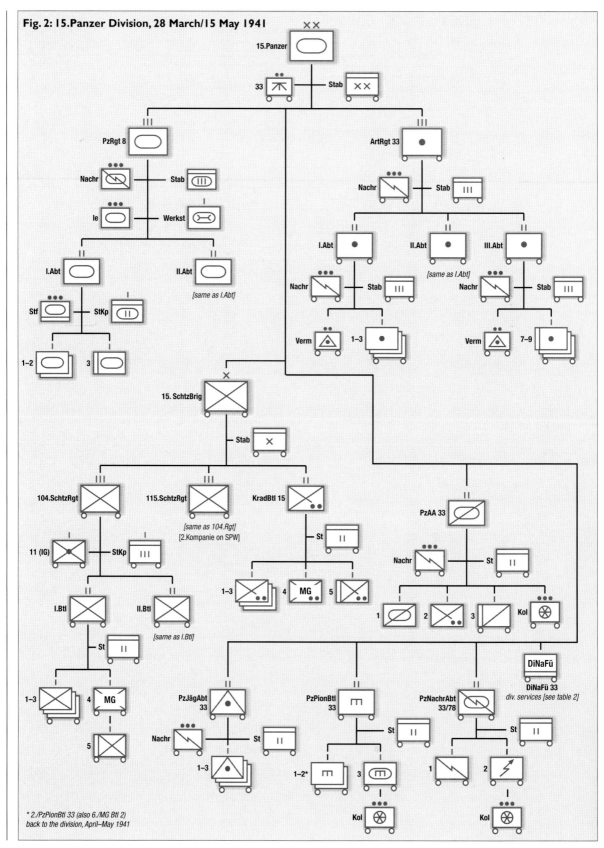

Fig. 2: 15.Panzer Division, 28 March/15 May 1941

Table 2: 15.Panzer Division, 28 March/15 May 1941

Generalmajor Heinrich von Prittwitz, from 15 April Generalmajor Hans-Karl von Esebeck

Stab (mot)

Div.Kartenstelle 33 (mot)

Panzer Rgt. 8

Stab

Panzer Nachrichtenzug

leichte Panzerzug

Panzerwerkstatt Kompanie

I.Abteilung

    Stabskompanie

    1.–2.leichte Panzerkompanie

    3.mittlere Panzerkompanie

    Panzer Staffel

II.Abteilung

    Stabskompanie

    5.–6.leichte Panzerkompanie

    7.mittlere Panzerkompanie

    Panzer Staffel

15.Schützen Brigade (mot)

Stab

104.Schützen Rgt. (mot)

    Stabskompanie (mot)

    I.Bataillon (mot)

        Stab (mot)

        1.–3.Schützen Kp. (mot)

        4.MG Kompanie (mot)

        5.schwere Kompanie (mot)

    II.Bataillon (mot)

        Stab (mot)

        6.–8.Schützen Kp. (mot)

        9.MG Kompanie (mot)

        10.schwere Kompanie (mot)

        11.Infanterie Geschütz Kp. (mot)

115.Schützen Rgt. (mot)

    Stabskompanie (mot)

    I.Bataillon (mot)

        Stab (mot)

        1.–3.Schützen Kp. (mot)

        4.MG Kompanie (mot)

        5.schwere Kompanie (mot)

    II.Bataillon (mot)

        Stab (mot)

        6.–8.Schützen Kp. (mot)

        9.MG Kompanie (mot)

        10.schwere Kompanie (mot)

        11.Infanterie Geschütz Kp. (mot) *

Kradschützen Bataillon 15 (mot)

    Stab (mot)

    1.–3.Kradschützen Kp. (mot)

    4.Krad. MG Kompanie (mot)

    5.schwere Kompanie (mot)

Artillerie Rgt. 33 (mot)

Stab (mot)

Nachrichtenzug (mot)

I.Abteilung (mot)

    Stab (mot)

    Nachrichtenzug (mot)

    Vermessungstrupp (mot)

    1.–3.leichte Batterie (mot)

II.Abteilung (mot)

    Stab (mot)

    Nachrichtenzug (mot)

    Vermessungstrupp (mot)

    4.–6.leichte Batterie (mot)

III.Abteilung (mot)

    Stab (mot)

    Nachrichtenzug (mot)

    Vermessungstrupp (mot)

    7.–9.schwere Batterie (mot)

Pz.Aufklärungs Abt. 33 (mot)

Stab (mot)

Nachrichtenzug (mot)

1.Panzerspäh Komp. (mot)

2.Kradschützen Kp. (mot)

3.schwere Kompanie (mot)

leichte Kolonne (mot)

(continues on page 18)

Panzerjäger Abt. 33 (mot)

Stab (mot)

Nachrichtenzug (mot)

1.–3.Panzerjäger Komp. (mot)

Pz.Pionier Bataillon 33 (mot)

Stab (mot)

1.–2.leichte Pionier Kompanie (mot) **

3.Pz. Pionier Kompanie

leichte Kolonne (mot)

Pz.Nachrichten Abt. 33/78 (mot) *

Stab (mot)

1.Nachrichten Kp. (mot)

2.Funk Kompanie (mot)

leichte Kolonne (mot)

Div.Nachschub Führer 33 (mot)

Stab (mot)

Kleine Kw Kolonne 1–7, 11–13/33 (mot)

Kw.Kol. für Betr.Stoff 8-10, 14/33 (mot)

[Gr.Kw.Kol. 13–14/33 (mot)] + Werkstatt Komp. 1–3/33 (mot)

Nachschub Kp. 33 (mot)

[Panzer Ersatzteilkolonne 33 (mot)] +

Divisions Verpflegungsamt 33 (mot)

Bäckerei Kompanie 33 (mot)

Schlachterei Kompanie 33 (mot)

Sanitäts Kompanie 1-2/33 (mot)

Feldlazarett 33 (mot)

Krankenkraftwagenzug 1–3/33 (mot)

Feldgendarmerietrupp 33 (mot)

Feldpostamt 33 (mot)

Notes
* sunk en-route and lost. Pz.Nachr.Abt. 33 was replaced by Pz.Nachr.Abt. 78
** 2./Pz.Pion.Btl. 33 back from MG Btl. 2, April–May and since May 1941

guns – were required. 5.leichte Division (soon to be renamed 21.Panzer Division) was to reach full divisional status with the addition of a *Schützen Brigade,* and a new motorized infantry division – the Afrika Division, with three infantry and one artillery regiments – was to be formed from available corps troops. These, however, had to be re-equipped and grouped under regimental HQs. Summing up, Rommel's requests included: two *Panzer Abteilungen,* four *Panzer Kompanien,* 55 *Infanterie* and *Pionier Kompanien,* several regimental and

A 150mm schwere Feldhaubitze 18 howitzer towed by an 8-ton Krauss-Maffei KM m 11 SdKfz 7 tractor (note the three external wheels). It belonged to III.Abteilung of either Artillerie Regiment 155 or 33. (Carlo Pecchi Collection)

battalion HQs, numerous armoured personnel carriers and an array of combat and support units. Understandably, the OKH rejected most of these requests and only agreed to the creation of the Afrika Division, for which only one regimental HQ and some infantry companies were available.

As both 21.Panzer Division and 15.Panzer Division were unbalanced with their current organization, some improvements were made by reshuffling their subordinate units. This occurred shortly after 5.leichte's renaming as 21.Panzer Division on 1 August 1941. This reorganization, mostly a paper exercise, affected divisional artillery and support units; Stab Artillerie Regiment 155 (mot), formed in Germany on 31 May 1941, was subordinated to 21.Panzer Division along with two *Artillerie Abteilungen* (schwere Artillerie Abteilung 864 becoming I./Artillerie Regiment 155, and schwere Artillerie Abteilung 911 becoming III./Artillerie Regiment 155), while I./Artillerie Regiment 75 became II./Artillerie Regiment 155. The latter remained the only artillery unit with the division since the Stab and both I. and III./Abteilung Artillerie Regiment 155 only arrived in North Africa between late October and late November 1941. Also, on 1 August 1941 the Panzer Nachrichten Abteilung 200, which absorbed the 3./Panzer Nachrichten Abteilung 39, and the Feldersatz Bataillon 200 were formed in Germany.

On 15 August 1941 the Stab of Panzergruppe Afrika was formed and placed under Rommel's command, thus formalizing the chain of command in North Africa. Ten days later this unit issued a note to the OKH stating that infantry battalions under its direct command could not be motorized, and therefore could not be used to strengthen 21.Panzer Division. As a consequence, to obtain a more balanced *Kampfkraft* (combat strength), Panzergruppe Afrika requested authorization to carry out the following organizational changes: Schützen Regiment 104 was to be subordinated to 21.Panzer Division and was to incorporate MG Bataillon 8, while both Schützen Regiment Stab zbV 200 and MG Bataillon 2 were to be subordinated to 15.Panzer Division's 15.Schützen Brigade, the former creating a regiment when combined with Kradschützen Bataillon 15. The OKH not only authorized these changes but, on 22 August, also ordered the creation of a fourth *Panzer Kompanie* in each *Panzer Abteilung*. Finally, 11.(IG)/Schützen Regiment 115 was to be rebuilt. The results of these changes (**Figs. 3** and **4**) were that 15.Panzer Division had now four rather than five infantry battalions, though its established strength was not much reduced (about 14,000), while 21.Panzer Division now had three rather than two infantry battalions (with a slight increase in overall established

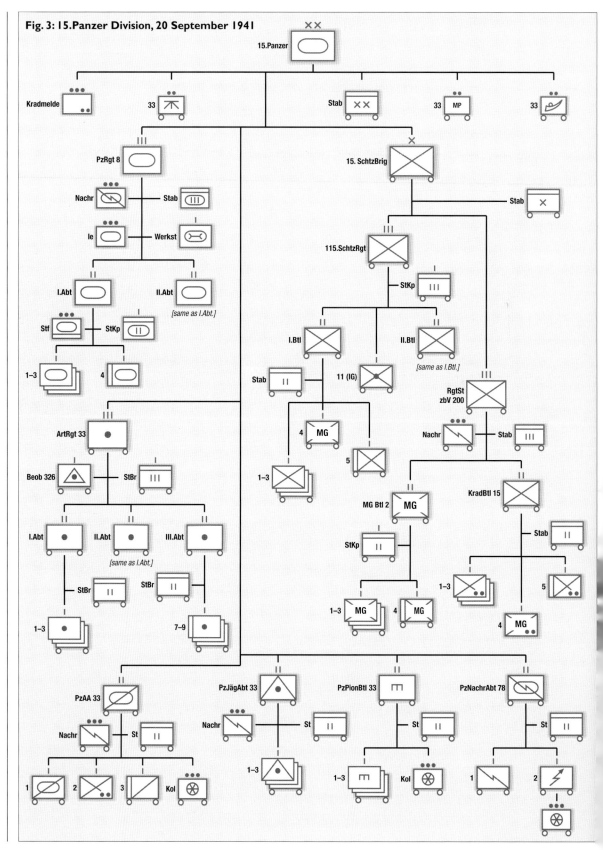

Fig. 3: 15.Panzer Division, 20 September 1941

Table 3: 15.Panzer Division, 20 September 1941

Generalmajor Walter Neumann-Silkow

Stab (mot)

Div.Kartenstelle 33 (mot)

Kradmeldezug

Panzer Rgt. 8

Stab

Panzer Nachrichtenzug

leichte Panzerzug

Panzerwerkstatt Kompanie

I.Abteilung

    Stabskompanie

    1.–3.leichte Panzerkompanie *

    4.mittlere Panzerkompanie

    Panzer Staffel

II.Abteilung

    Stabskompanie

    5.–7.leichte Panzerkompanie *

    8.mittlere Panzerkompanie

    Panzer Staffel

15.Schützen Brigade (mot)

Stab

115. Schützen Rgt. (mot)

    Stabskompanie (mot)

    I.Bataillon (mot)

        Stab (mot)

        1., 3.Schützen Kp. (mot)

        2.Schützen Kp. (gep)

        4.MG Kompanie (mot)

        5.schwere Kompanie (mot)

    II.Bataillon (mot)

        Stab (mot)

        6.–8.Schützen Kp. (mot)

        9.MG Kompanie (mot)

        10.schwere Kompanie (mot)

        11. Infanterie Geschütz Kp. (mot) [reforming]

Rgt Stab zbV 200 (mot)

    Stab (mot)

    Nachrichtenzug (mot)

    MG Bataillon 2 (mot)

    Stabskompanie (mot)

    1.–3.MG Schützen Kp. (mot)

    4.schwere Kompanie (mot)

Kradschützen Bataillon 15 (mot)

    Stab (mot)

    1.–3.Kradschützen Kp. (mot)

    4.Krad. MG Kompanie (mot)

    5.schwere Kompanie (mot)

Artillerie Rgt. 33 (mot)

Stabsbatterie (mot)

Beobachtungs Batterie 326 (mot)

I.Abteilung (mot)

    Stabsbatterie (mot)

    1.–3.leichte Batterie (mot)

II.Abteilung (mot)

    Stabsbatterie (mot)

    4.–6.leichte Batterie (mot)

III.Abteilung (mot)

    Stabsbatterie (mot)

    7.–9.schwere Batterie (mot)

Pz.Aufklärungs Abt. 33 (mot)

Stab (mot)

Nachrichtenzug (mot)

1.Panzerspäh Komp. (mot)

2.Kradschützen Kp. (mot)

3.schwere Kompanie (mot)

leichte Kolonne (mot)

Panzerjäger Abt. 33 (mot)

Stab (mot)

Nachrichtenzug (mot)

1.–3.Panzerjäger Komp. (mot)

Pz.Pionier Bataillon 33 (mot)

Stab (mot)

1.–3.Pionier Kompanie (mot)

leichte Kolonne (mot)

(continues on page 22)

Pz.Nachrichten Abt. 78 (mot)

Stab (mot)
1.Nachrichten Kp. (mot)
2.Funk Kompanie (mot)
leichte Kolonne (mot)

Feldersatz Bataillon 33

1.–3.Kompanie

Div.Nachschub Führer 33 (mot)

Stab (mot)
Kleine Kw Kolonne 1–7, 12/33 (mot)
Grosse Kraftwagenkolonne 13–14/33 (mot)
Kw.Kol. für Betr.Stoff 8–10/33 (mot)
Werkstatt Komp. 1–3/33 (mot)
Nachschub Kp. 33 (mot)
Panzer Ersatzteilkolonne 33 (mot)
Filtergerätkolonne 33 (mot)
Leichte Wasserkolonne 33 (mot)

Divisions Verpflegungsamt 33 (mot)
Bäckerei Kompanie 33 (mot)
Schlachterei Kompanie 33 (mot)
Sanitäts Kompanie 1–2/33 (mot)
Feldlazarett 36 (mot)
Krankenkraftwagenzug 1–2/33 (mot)
Feldgendarmerietrupp 33 (mot)
Feldpostamt 33 (mot)

* 3. and 7.leichte Panzerkompanie in the process of forming.

strength, now about 13,000, but with a decisive increase in infantry strength). The reorganization of the *Panzer Abteilungen* was longer and more complicated; Panzer Regiment 8 re-designated its 3rd and 7th companies as *leichte Panzer Kompanien* and raised both 4. and 8.mittlere Panzer Kompanie from scratch. On the other hand, Panzer Regiment 5 simply created a new 3. and 7.leichte Panzer Kompanie. In both cases, however, the reorganization took a great deal of time; new companies began to be formed only in November 1941, and they did not appear in permanent establishments until February/March 1942.

Meanwhile, the reorganization also affected corps troops and the newly formed Divisions Kommando zbV Afrika. On 24 August Fla Bataillon 612 (mot) was formed, eventually joining Fla Bataillon 606 (sfl) and the two Luftwaffe Flak *Abteilungen* as Panzergruppe Afrika's anti-aircraft force. On 15 September three of the five *Stellungsbataillone* (static infantry battalions) under Panzergruppe Afrika's command were grouped together forming Schützen Regiment 155, whose Stab had been formed in Germany in early June. This unit consisted of III./Infanterie Regiment 241 (renamed I./SR 155), III./IR 258 (renamed II./SR 155) and III./IR 268 (renamed III./SR 155), while the two remaining battalions remained unattached. In the meantime new units had joined the Panzergruppe:

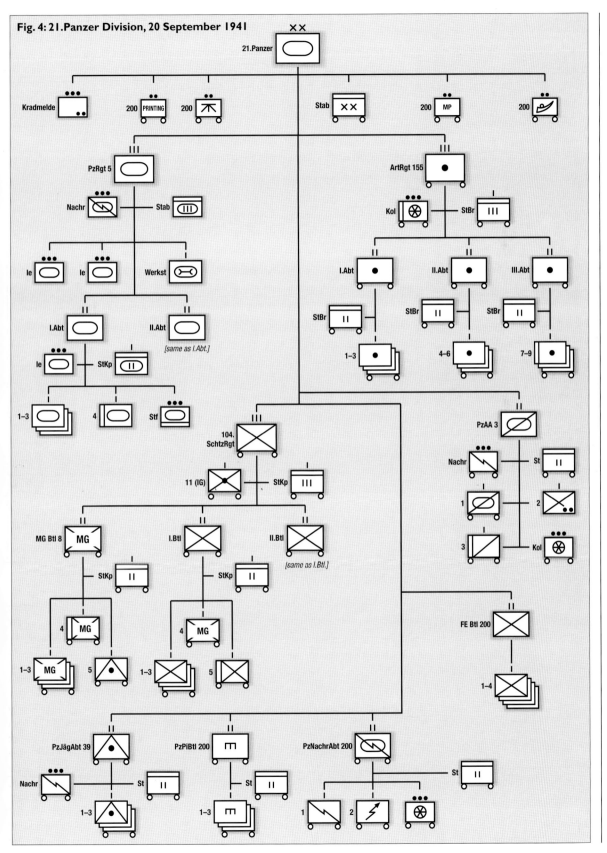

Fig. 4: 21.Panzer Division, 20 September 1941

Table 4: 21.Panzer Division, 20 September 1941

Generalmajor Johann von Ravenstein

Stab (mot)

Div.Kartenstelle 200 (mot)

Drückereitrupp 200 (mot)

Kradmeldezug

Panzer Rgt. 5

Stab

Panzer Nachrichtenzug

leichte Panzerzug

leichte Panzerzug

Panzerwerkstatt Kompanie

I.Abteilung

   Stabskompanie

   leichte Panzerzug

   1.–3. leichte Panzerkompanie *

   4. mittlere Panzerkompanie

   Panzer Staffel

II.Abteilung

   Stabskompanie

   leichte Panzerzug

   5.–7. leichte Panzerkompanie *

   8.mittlere Panzerkompanie

   Panzer Staffel

104. Schützen Rgt. (mot)

Stabskompanie (mot)

I.Bataillon (mot)

   Stab (mot)

   1.–3.Schützen Kp. (mot)

   4.MG Kompanie (mot)

   5.schwere Kompanie (mot)

II.Bataillon (mot)

   Stab (mot)

   6.–8.Schützen Kp. (mot)

   9.MG Kompanie (mot)

   10.schwere Kompanie (mot)

11.Infanterie Geschütz Kp. (mot)

MG Bataillon 8 (mot)

   Stabskompanie (mot)

   1.–3.MG Schützen Kp. (mot)

4.schwere Kompanie (mot)

5.Panzerjäger Kp. (mot)

Artillerie Rgt. 155 (mot)

Stabsbatterie (mot)

Schwere Artillerie Kolonne (mot)

I.Abteilung (mot)

   Stabsbatterie (mot)

   1.–3.leichte Batterie (mot)

II.Abteilung (mot) **

   Stabsbatterie (mot)

   4.–6.leichte Batterie (mot)

III.Abteilung (mot)

   Stabsbatterie (mot)

   7.–9.schwere Batterie (mot)

Pz.Aufklärungs Abt. 3 (mot)

Stab (mot)

Nachrichtenzug (mot)

1.Panzerspäh Komp. (mot)

2.Kradschützen Kp. (mot)

3.schwere Kompanie (mot)

leichte Kolonne (mot)

Panzerjäger Abt. 39 (mot)

Stab (mot)

Nachrichtenzug (mot)

1.–3.Panzerjäger Komp. (mot)

Pz.Pionier Bataillon 200 (mot)

Stab (mot)

1.–3.Pionier Kompanie (mot)

Pz.Nachrichten Abt. 200 (mot)

Stab (mot)

1.Nachrichten Kp. (mot)

2.Funk Kompanie (mot)

leichte Kolonne (mot)

24 | *(continues on page 25)*

Feldersatz Bataillon 200

Stab

1.–4.Kompanie

Div.Nachschub Führer 200 (mot)

Stab (mot)

Gr.Kraftwagenkolonne 1–2, 10–11/200 (mot)

Kleine Kw Kolonne 3–8, 12/200 (mot)

Große Kw.Kol. für Betr.Stoff 9/200 (mot)

Werkstatt Komp. 1/200 (mot)

Kfz.Inst. Komp. 2–3/200 (mot)

Pz.Ersatzteilkolonne 200 (mot)

Nachschub Kp. 200 (mot)

Filterkolonne 200 (mot)

Leichte Wasserkolonne 200 (mot)

Divisions Verpflegungsamt 200 (mot)

Bäckerei Kompanie 200 (mot)

Schlachterei Kompanie 200 (mot)

Sanitäts Kompanie 1–2/200 (mot)

Feldlazarett 200 (mot)

Krankenkraftwagenzug 1–2/200 (mot)

Feldgendarmerietrupp 200 (mot)

Feldpostamt 200 (mot)

* 3. and 7.leichte Panzerkompanien in the process of forming

** II./Art.Rgt. 155 from I./Art.Rgt. 75

the Stab of Artillerie Kommandeur 104 and of Artillerie Regiment 221, two *Heeres Küsten Artillerie Abteilungen* (army coastal artillery) plus five batteries, Panzer Nachrichten Regiment 10, two *Feldersatz Bataillone* and Aufklärungs Kompanie 580. Also, on 19 September, the schwere Infanterie Geschütz Kompanien (sfl) 707 and 708 were formed according to an OKH order.

On 26 June 1941 the OKH had ordered the creation of the Stab Divisions Kommando zbV Afrika, which was formed in Germany by mid-July. However, since DAK's requests of late July were rejected by the OKH, it was soon clear this HQ was not needed to create the motorized infantry division deemed necessary to support the other two. Therefore, it fell well down in the transportation list and was only sent to North Africa between late August and late September 1941, when it took over command in the Sollum area. The first units were attached on 15 October 1941, initially for training purposes only, and were III./IR 347 and Bataillon zbV 300 'Oasen'. Two weeks later 21.Panzer's I./Schützen Regiment 104 (temporarily subordinated to the Afrika Division itself) replaced it at Sollum. On 20 October more units, formerly corps troops, followed: Schützen Regiment 155, III./IR 255, Pionier Bataillon 900 and Panzerjäger Abteilung 605. Afrika Regiment 361 was also subordinated to the division. This unit, which was composed of former French Foreign Legion veterans (and was not considered completely reliable), had

A PzKpfw III (very likely an early or mid-production Ausf. G) belonging to the Stab of I.Abteilung in either Panzer Regiment 5 or 8. It was a common practice for HQ vehicles to sport pennants, although the one shown here is atypical since it displays the Panzerwaffe's death's-head insignia. (Carlo Pecchi Collection)

A crowd of mixed DAK vehicles somewhere in the desert in mid-1941. Amongst the many vehicles shown there are a PzKpfw I Ausf. A, several Opel Blitz 3-ton lorries, a Demag D7 SdKfz 10 towing a very large trailer, a lonely Kübelwagen, a captured British Chevrolet lorry and an Italian TL 37 light tractor (left, close to the pole). Note how the German vehicles have a coat of sand paint over the dark-grey original layer, which can be seen on DAK's insignia. (Carlo Pecchi Collection)

been formed in Germany on 15 June and arrived in North Africa between 20 October and mid-November. It was immediately deployed at Belhamed along with SR 155 while, at the same time, both III./IR 255 and III./IR 347 moved to Bardia to complete their training. At this point, Rommel decided that Afrika Division zbV (as it was known then) was to lead the planned attack against the fortress of Tobruk and ordered its redeployment to Bardia. On 2 November all the above-listed units (with the exception of Panzerjäger Abteilung 605) were subordinated to the Stab Divisions Kommando zbV Afrika, followed a week later by the Stab and II Abteilung of AR 155, 11.(IG)/SR 104 and Aufklärungs Kompanie 580, all temporarily attached like I./SR 104. On 15 November 1941 Rommel ordered that Afrika Division zbV was to replace the Italian division 'Bologna' east of Tobruk and that all the units not yet in the Belhamed area had to be moved there by the 20th. Two days before, the British had launched Operation *Crusader*. Finally, on 28 November, the division was renamed 90.leichte Afrika Division (**Fig. 5**).

Fig. 5: Afrika Division zbV (From 28 November 1941 90.leichte Afrika)

(Units attached from other divisions are excluded)

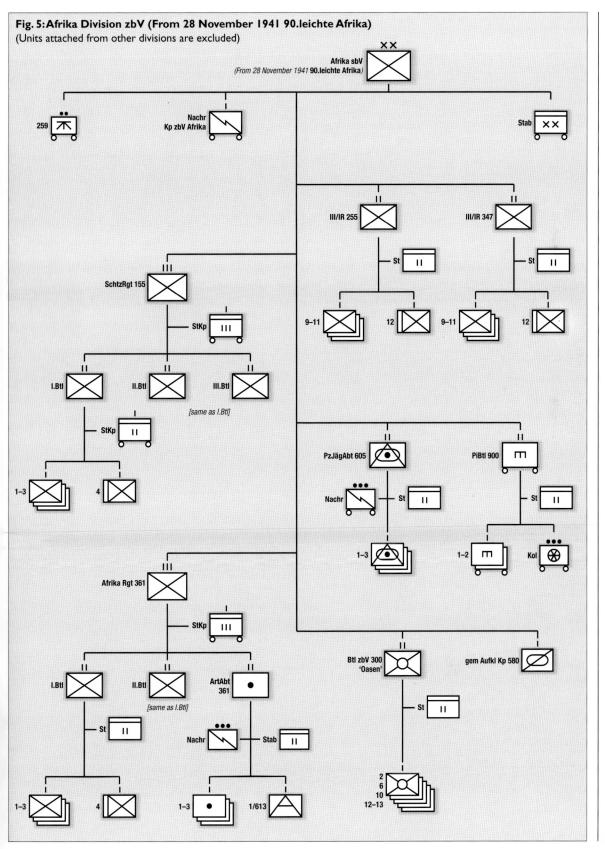

Table 5: Afrika Division zbV, 10 November 1941

(From 28 November 90.leichte Afrika Division)

Generalmajor Max Sümmermann

Stab (mot)	**III./Infanterie Regiment 255**
Div.Kartenstelle 259 (mot)	Stab
Nachrichten Kompanie zbV Afrika (mot)	9.–11.Infanterie Kompanie
	12.MG Kompanie
Schützen Rgt. 155	
Stabskompanie (mot)	**III./Infanterie Regiment 347**
I.Bataillon	Stab
Stabskompanie	9.–11.Infanterie Kompanie
1.–3.Schützen Kp.	12.MG Kompanie
4.MG Kompanie	
II.Bataillon	**Panzerjäger Abt. 605 (sfl)**
Stabskompanie	Stab (mot)
6.–8.Schützen Kp.	Nachrichtenzug (mot)
9.MG Kompanie	1.–3. Panzerjäger Komp. (sfl)
III.Bataillon	
Stabskompanie	**Pionier Bataillon 900 (mot)**
11.–13.Schützen Kp.	Stab (mot)
14.MG Kompanie	1.–2.Pionier Kompanie (mot)
	leichte Kolonne (mot)
Afrika Regiment 361	
Stab	**Bataillon zbV 300 'Oasen'**
I.Bataillon	Stab
Stab	2., 6., 10., 12.–13.'Oasen' Kompanie
1.–3.Afrika Infanterie Kp.	
4.MG Kompanie	**gemischte Aufklärungs Kp. 580 ****
II.Bataillon	* 1./613 Fla Kp. is shown in organization charts from December 1941, 3./Art.Abt. 361 from February 1942
Stab	** permanently attached on 17 January 1942
5.–7.Afrika Infanterie Kp.	
8.MG Kompanie	
Artillerie Abteilung 361 *	
Stab	
Nachrichtenzug	
1.–3. Batterie	
1./613 Fla Kompanie	

Heavy losses were suffered during Operation *Crusader*. As a consequence, some units were completely lost (III./IR 255, Bataillon zbV 300 'Oasen' and I./SR 104, which surrendered at Sollum in January 1942), while others were badly mauled. At the end of December 1941, 15.Panzer Division had lost at least five companies plus the Stab of Schützen Regiment 115, the Kradschützen Bataillon 15 was down to a single company, Artillerie Regiment 33 had lost four batteries and its

III.Abteilung was down to cadres, while Panzer Pionier Bataillon 33 had lost its Stab and two out of three companies. The situation was such that Regiments Stab zbV 200 was temporarily disbanded while MG Bataillon 2, along with the remnants of Kradschützen Bataillon 15 and Panzer Pionier Bataillon 33, were merged and put under the direct command of 15.Schützen Brigade. 21.Panzer Division was in no better shape; Panzer Regiment 5 had to be withdrawn and re-equipped, the artillery component was reduced to four batteries (III./AR 155 had been almost wiped out), Panzerjäger Abteilung 39 was down to two companies and Panzer Pionier Bataillon 200 was reduced to a single one. The situation was even worse for 90.leichte Afrika Division, which, left with only a dozen infantry companies, had two newly arrived infantry units attached – Sonderverband 288 and Kampfgruppe Burckhardt, a *Fallschirmjäger* unit formed from XI Fliegerkorps' Fallschirm Lehr Bataillon (for this and other *Fallschirmjäger* units see Bruce Quarrie's *Battle Orders 15: German Airborne Divisions: The Mediterranean Theatre 1942–45*, Osprey Publishing Ltd: Oxford, 2005). Thanks to a quick recovery, in late January 1942 Panzerarmee Afrika (as it was renamed on 22 January) started a new drive into Cyrenaica that eventually stopped in early February in front of Gazala. By this stage a major reorganization was badly needed.

As opposed to the July 1941 reorganization, this time experience played its part and senior commanders had their voices heard. During a discussion with Rommel in January 1942, Generalmajor Richard Veith (commander of 90.leichte Afrika Division) criticized the current organization of infantry battalions. He suggested they should be composed of four balanced companies, each one having its own heavy weapons and anti-tank guns, as opposed to three infantry and one heavy company. In the same month Generalleutnant Gustav von Vaerst, commander of 15.Panzer Division, sent Rommel a proposal that focused on the strengthening of Panzer and artillery units. He also proposed a reduction in the number of infantry, with a commensurate increase in the both the number and quality of weapons and equipment (in particular vehicles). Many of these proposals could not be accepted by the OKH, and Rommel rejected them. Some points had been decided upon. Firstly, organization was to hinge on the principle of 'more weapons, less men', partly as a result of the heavy losses incurred. Secondly, divisions and subordinate units had to be more balanced, in particular as to the allocation of anti-tank weapons. Therefore, on 14 February 1942 the Panzerarmee sent a new proposal to the OKH suggesting a new, major reorganization. This focused mainly on infantry (each Panzer division was to have a three-battalion *Schützen Regiment*) and reconnaissance units, as well as proposing the creation of a second motorized infantry division. OKH's reply of 10 March rejected the latter, but authorized all the other proposals. Eventually, on 28 March the Panzerarmee ordered a definitive reorganization for all its subordinate divisions. Tables of organization and equipment were updated and, effective from 1 April, a final reshuffling took place: 15.Panzer Division gave its Kradschützen Bataillon 15 to 21.Panzer Division, which also permanently incorporated Schützen Regiment 104. Stab Schützen Regiment 200 and 1./Panzerjäger Abteilung 33 were given to 90.leichte Afrika Division, and the Stab 15.Schützen Brigade was subordinated directly to the Panzerarmee. MG Bataillon 2, already attached, was disbanded and used to form III./Schützen Regiment 115. Within 21.Panzer Division, Schützen Regiment 104 was rebuilt with both Kradschützen Bataillon 15 (becoming III./SR 104) and MG Bataillon 8 (becoming I./Schützen Regiment 104) apart from 5.(Pz.Jäg.) Kompanie, which was given to 90.Afrika Division.

From 1 April 1942, 15. and 21.Panzer Division shared a similar organizational structure (**Figs. 6** and **7**). Each had a two-battalion Panzer regiment and a three-battalion *Schützen Regiment*, whose companies – all identical – had been formed through the merging of the former *Schützen*, *MG* and *schwere Kompanien*. Moreover, a 13.(Infanterie Geschütz) and a 14.(Pionier) Kompanie were added. The attempt to strengthen the *Panzer Aufklärungs Abteilung* by adding a second

Table 6: 15.Panzer Division, 1 May 1942

(Generalleutnant Gustav von Vaerst)

Stab (mot)

Div.Kartenstelle 33 (mot)

Panzer Befehlsstaffel

Panzer Rgt. 8

Stab

Panzer Nachrichtenzug

Leichte Panzerzug

Panzerwerkstatt Kompanie

I.Abteilung

   Stabskompanie

   1.–3.leichte Panzerkompanie

   4.mittlere Panzerkompanie

   Panzer Staffel

II.Abteilung

   Stabskompanie

   5.–7.leichte Panzerkompanie

   8.mittlere Panzerkompanie

   Panzer Staffel

Schützen Rgt. 115 (mot) *

Stabskompanie (mot)

I.Bataillon (mot)

   Stab (mot)

   1.–4.Schützen Kp. (mot)

II.Bataillon (mot)

   Stab (mot)

   5.–8.Schützen Kp. (mot)

II. Bataillon (mot)

   Stab (mot)

   9.–12.Schützen Kp. (mot)

13.Infanterie Geschütz Kp. (mot)

14.Pionier Kompanie (mot)

Pz.Aufklärungs Abt. 33 (mot)

Stab (mot)

1.Panzerspäh Komp. (mot)

2.leichte Schützen Späh Kompanie (mot)

3.schwere Kompanie (mot)

4.(Beute) Batterie (mot)

leichte Kolonne (mot)

Panzerjäger Abt. 33 (mot)

Stab (mot)

Nachrichtenzug (mot)

1.–2.Panzerjäger Komp. (mot) **

Pz.Pionier Bataillon 33 (mot)

Stab (mot)

1.–3.Pionier Kompanie (mot)

leichte Kolonne (mot)

Pz.Nachrichten Abt. 78 (mot)

Stab (mot)

1.Pz. Nachrichten Kp. (mot)

2.Pz. Funk Kompanie (mot)

leichte Kolonne (mot)

Artillerie Rgt. 33 (mot) **

Stabsbatterie (mot)

Beobachtungs Batterie 33 (mot)

Schwere Kolonne (mot)

I.Abteilung (mot)

   Stabsbatterie (mot)

   1.–3.leichte Batterie (mot)

II.Abteilung (mot)

   Stabsbatterie (mot)

   4.–6.leichte Batterie (mot)

III.Abteilung (mot)

   Stabsbatterie (mot)

   7.–9.schwere Batterie (mot)

Feldersatz Bataillon 33

1.–4.Kompanie

Div.Nachschub Führer 33 (mot)

Stab (mot)

Kleine Kw Kolonne 1–8/33 (mot)

 (continues on page 31)

Grosse Kraftwagenkolonne 13–14/33 (mot)
Kw.Kol. für Betr.Stoff 10–12/33 (mot)
Werkstatt Komp. 1–3/33 (mot)
Nachschub Kp. 33 (mot)
Panzer Ersatzteilkolonne 33 (mot)
Grosse Wasserkolonne 33 (mot)
Filtergerätkolonne 33 (mot)

Divisions Verpflegungsamt 33 (mot)
Bäckerei Kompanie 33 (mot)
Schlachterei Kompanie 33 (mot)
Sanitäts Kompanie 1–2/33 (mot)
Feldlazarett 36 (mot)
Krankenkraftwagenzug 1–3/33 (mot)
Feldgendarmerietrupp 33 (mot)
Feldpostamt 33 (mot)

Attached after mid-April 1942:

I.Abteilung/Flak Regiment 43 (mot)
Stab (mot)
1.–3.leichte Flak Batterie (mot)
4.–5.schwere Flak Batterie (mot)

* became Panzergrenadier Regiment 115 after 5 July 1942 (sub-units renamed
    Panzergrenadier Bataillon and Kompanie)
** 1./Panzerjäger Abteilung 33 became self-propelled (sfl) in September 1942
*** became Panzer Artillerie Abteilung 33 after 15 July 1942 (sub-units renamed
    consequently)
Notes:
• 13.(IG) and 14.(Pi)Kompanie/Panzergrenadier Regiment 115 on paper only since August
    1942. A new 15.(Beute) Batterie is formed in the same month and renamed as such in
    September/October. In October 13.(IG)/PzGrenRgt 115 is reformed (from the schwere
    Infanterie Geschütz Kompanie 707?). Neither 13. nor 14.Kompanie were officially disbanded.
• Since 20 August 1942 a 10.(sfl) Batterie/Panzer Artillerie Regiment 33 was added.

Panzerspäh Kompanie failed, however, although the Kradschützen Kompanien were
equipped with armoured personnel carriers and transformed into Schützen Späh
Kompanien. Also, from mid-February, a fourth (Beute) Batterie was formed using
captured British 25-pdr guns. Heavy losses (3./Panzerjäger Abteilung 39 had to be
disbanded), increased need for the Schützen Kompanien and allocations to the
90.leichte Afrika Division also reduced to two the number of companies in the
Panzerjäger Abteilungen. By mid/late April each division also had a Fla or Flak unit
attached. All in all, established strengths dropped to about 11,000 for each Panzer
Division, though there was a considerable increase in weapons: about 200-odd
tanks (of which 160 medium) and 60 anti-tank guns, on paper at least.

On 1 April 90.leichte Afrika Division was also reorganized and renamed
90.leichte Infanterie Division (**Fig. 8**). Both Schützen Regiment 155 and Afrika
Regiment 361 were renamed and reorganized as leichte Infanterie Regimenter,
both with two four-company battalions (their organization matched that of the
Schützen Bataillon). III./SR 155 and III./IR 347 were subordinated to Stab

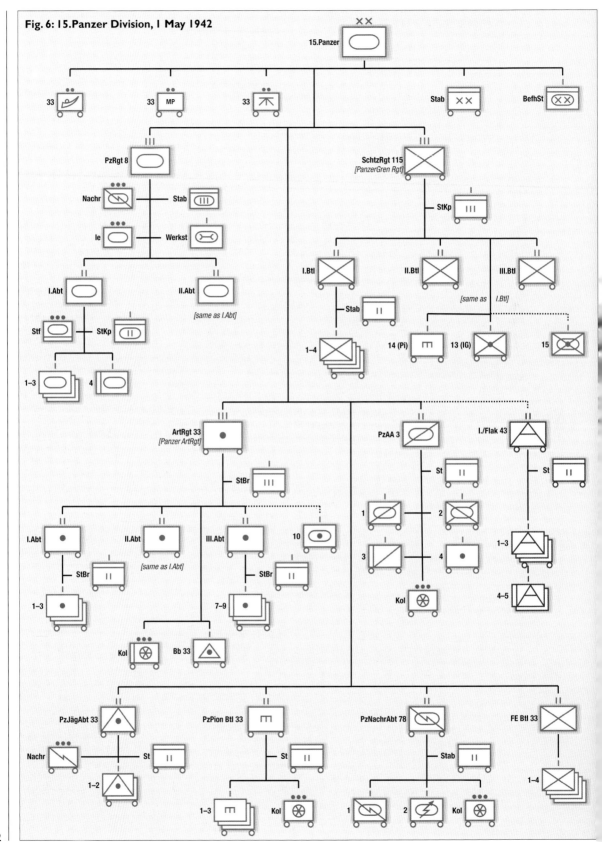

Fig. 6: 15.Panzer Division, 1 May 1942

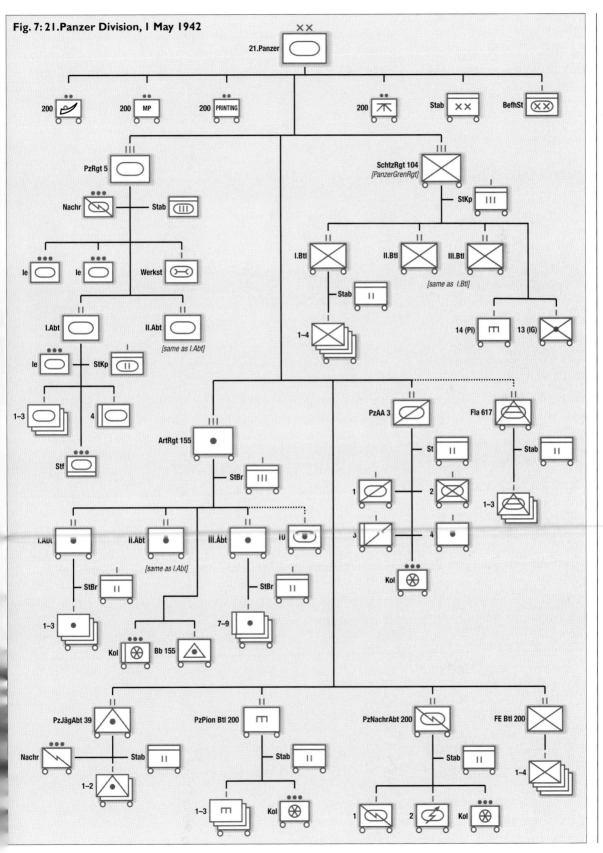

Fig. 7: 21.Panzer Division, 1 May 1942

Table 7: 21.Panzer Division, 1 May 1942

(Generalmajor Georg von Bismarck)

Stab (mot)

Div.Kartenstelle 200 (mot)

Drückereitrupp 200 (mot)

Panzer Befehlsstaffel

Panzer Rgt. 5

Stab

Panzer Nachrichtenzug

leichte Panzerzug

leichte Panzerzug

Panzerwerkstatt Kompanie

I.Abteilung

    Stabskompanie

    leichte Panzerzug

    1.–3.leichte Panzerkompanie

    4.mittlere Panzerkompanie

    Panzer Staffel

II.Abteilung

    Stabskompanie

    leichte Panzerzug

    5.–7.leichte Panzerkompanie

    8.mittlere Panzerkompanie

    Panzer Staffel

Schützen Rgt. 104 (mot) *

Stabskompanie (mot)

I.Bataillon (mot)

    Stab (mot)

    1.–4.Schützen Kp. (mot)

II.Bataillon (mot)

    Stab (mot)

    5.–8.Schützen Kp. (mot)

II.Bataillon (mot)

    Stab (mot)

    9.–12.Schützen Kp. (mot)

13.Infanterie Geschütz Kp. (mot)

14.Pionier Kompanie (mot)

Pz.Aufklärungs Abt. 3 (mot)

Stab (mot)

1.Panzerspäh Komp. (mot)

2.leichte Schützen Späh Kompanie (mot)

3.schwere Kompanie (mot)

4.(Beute) Batterie (mot)

leichte Kolonne (mot)

Panzerjäger Abt. 39 (mot)

Stab (mot)

Nachrichtenzug (mot)

1.–2.Panzerjäger Komp. (mot) **

Pz.Pionier Bataillon 200 (mot) +

Stab (mot)

1.–3.Pionier Kompanie (mot)

leichte Kolonne (mot)

Artillerie Rgt. 155 (mot) §

Stabsbatterie (mot)

Beobachtungs Batterie 155 (mot)

schwere Kolonne (mot)

I.Abteilung (mot)

    Stabsbatterie (mot)

    1.–3.leichte Batterie (mot)

II.Abteilung (mot)

    Stabsbatterie (mot)

    4.–6.leichte Batterie (mot)

III.Abteilung (mot)

    Stabsbatterie (mot)

    7.–9.schwere Batterie (mot)

Pz.Nachrichten Abt. 200 (mot)

Stab (mot)

1.Pz. Nachrichten Kp. (mot)

2.Pz. Funk Kompanie (mot)

leichte Kolonne (mot)

Feldersatz Bataillon 200

1.–4.Kompanie

 (continues on page 35)

Div.Nachschub Führer 200 (mot)

Stab (mot)

Kleine Kw Kolonne 1–8, 12/200 (mot)

Grosse Kraftwagenkolonne 10–11/200 (mot)

Kw.Kol. für Betr.Stoff 9/200 (mot)

Werkstatt Komp. 1/200 (mot)

Kfz.Inst. Komp. 2–3/200 (mot)

Nachschub Kp. 200 (mot)

Panzer Ersatzteilkolonne 200 (mot)

Grosse Wasserkolonne 645 (mot)

Filtergerätkolonne 200 (mot)

Divisions Verpflegungsamt 200 (mot)

Bäckerei Kompanie 200 (mot)

Schlachterei Kompanie 200 (mot)

Sanitäts Kompanie 1–2/200 (mot)

Feldlazarett 200 (mot)

Krankenkraftwagenzug 1–3/200 (mot)

Feldgendarmerietrupp 200 (mot)

Feldpostamt 200 (mot)

Attached from mid-April 1942:

Fla Bataillon 617 (sfl)

Stab (mot)

1.–3.Fla Kompanie (sfl)

* became Panzergrenadier Regiment 104 after 15 July 1942 (sub-units renamed Panzergrenadier Bataillon and Kompanie)

** 1./Panzerjäger Abteilung 39 became self-propelled (sfl) in September 1942

§ became Panzer Artillerie Regiment 155 after 15 July 1942 (sub-units renamed consequently)

+ Down to 1.–2. Kompanie from August 1942

Notes:

• 14.(Pi) Kompanie/Panzergrenadier Regiment 104 existed on paper only after August 1942. In September the same fate apparently befell 13.(IG)/Kompanie, which might have been replaced by schwere Infanterie Geschütz Kompanie 708 (it is uncertain as to whether 14.Kompanie was rebuilt in the same month). Neither 13. nor 14.Kompanie were officially disbanded.

• After 20 August 1942 10.(sfl) Batterie/Panzer Artillerie Regiment 155 was added.

Rommel's Kampfstaffel

Rommel's 'combat detachment' was formed in February 1942 when many captured tanks were available after the second drive into Cyrenaica. Although Rommel approved the creation of a *Beute Panzerabteilung* equipped with American M3 Honey and British Crusader tanks, only a single company was formed. Nevertheless, it provided the core of the Kasta (short for Kampstaffel), formed in March/April 1942 with a first *Panzerjäger Kompanie* and a second (*Beute*) *Panzerkompanie*. The former had three 50mm Pak and eight self-propelled light Flak guns, while the latter was equipped with 12 Crusader and two Honeys tanks. Shortly before the Gazala offensive, Rommel reorganized the Kasta by merging these two companies in a single one and by adding two new companies: one of infantry from 13./Lehr Regiment Brandenburg zbV 800 (also known as Kompanie von Koenen), and 3. Kompanie 1./Flak Abteilung 43. All in all, the strength of the Kasta strength was about 530 all ranks and its armament included four Crusader and one Honey tanks, one 25-pdr gun, three 50mm and one 75mm Pak, ten 20mm and eight 88mm Flak guns. As such it proved extremely valuable as a small, but effective, fighting unit directly subordinated to Rommel.

Schützen Regiment 200 to form leichte Infanterie Regiment 200, while one of the *schwere Infanterie Geschütz Kompanien* already under Panzerarmee's command was attached to each regiment (a third one was to come from 13./Schützen Regiment 115). Panzerjäger Abteilung 190 was formed using two companies from 15. and 21.Panzer Division and a Stab that had been formed in Germany, while in early May gemischte Aufklärungs Kompanie 580 was upgraded to a full *Aufklärungs Abteilung*, whose organization matched that of a Panzer division's *Panzer Aufklärungs Abteilung*. Artillerie Regiment 190 began forming in Germany with its II.Abteilung (the first being provided by Artillerie

Abteilung 361), although it – like Panzer Abteilung 190 –, never joined the division; instead they landed in Tunisia in November 1942. In spite of the creation by mid-May of a divisional support staff, supply and support units were meagre until mid-August. Overall established strength was still weak and some other units had to be attached by mid-April; these consisted of Panzerjäger Abteilung 605, Fla Bataillon 606 and Sonderverband 288. By mid-May 1942, 90.leichte's Division's established strength was about 12,500, though it eventually rose to about 14,500 by mid-August.

Changes were introduced only to a limited degree in the months to come. In August/September 1942 15. and 21.Panzer Division's *Panzergrenadier Regimenter* (as the *Schützen Regimenter* had been renamed in late July following an OKH order) lost their 13.(Infanterie Geschütz) and 14.(Pionier) Kompanien, although these were not officially disbanded. In September/ October Panzergrenadier Regiment 115 eventually rebuilt its 14.(Pionier) Kompanie and formed a new 15.(Beute) Batterie, while schwere Infanterie Geschütz Kompanien 707 and 708 were used to make good the loss of 13.Kompanie. On 20 August 10.(sfl) Batterie was formed by both *Panzer Artillerie Regimenter* following an order from OKH, though their actual creation depended on the piecemeal arrival of self-propelled guns. However, it was 90.leichte Division that underwent the most changes: between 1 July and 4 August it gained the Stab 15.Schützen Brigade, with leichte Infanterie Regiment 200 and 361 (IR 155 followed by mid-July). During the same period both IR 200 and 361 were fully motorized and, by August, the division finally reached its full complement. On 26 July, it reverted back to its old name of 90.leichte Afrika Division (also all its infantry units were redesignated Panzergrenadier).

In early July, following Panzerarmee Afrika's advance into Egypt (by then it was also known as the deutsch–italienische Panzerarmee, the German–Italian army), the decision was taken to form the Fallschirmjäger Brigade Ramcke with the aim of using it to establish a bridgehead across the Nile. It was composed of four selected *Fallschirmjäger* battalions, one of which, the Fallschirm Lehr Bataillon Burckhard, had already been in Africa the previous January and March. The bulk of the brigade arrived in Egypt in early August. Here it faced a quite different situation: the offensive had stopped and reinforcements were now needed to defend the Alamein Line. Two-thirds of the brigade had arrived by 20 August, and on 1 September it was redesignated Luftwaffen Jäger Brigade 1. Also, as early as mid-July, units of Festung Division 'Kreta' (formed in January 1942 from 164.Infanterie Division) were being hurried to Egypt by air to face the growing crisis. The order to transfer the bulk of the division followed by 20 July, and on 15 August a new division began to form in Egypt using both corps troops (Infanterie Regiment 125) and units from the Festung Division 'Kreta'. This

Fig. 8: 90.leichte Infanterie Division, 10 May 1942

(Intended and actual organization)

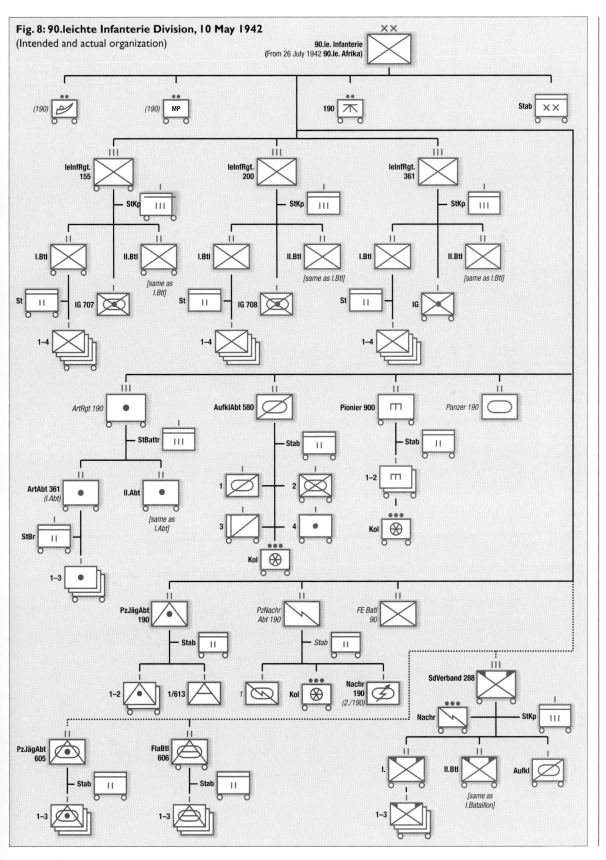

Table 8: 90.leichte Infanterie Division, 10 May 1942

[from 26 July 1942: 90.leichte Afrika Division]

(*Generalmajor Ulrich Kleeman*)

Stab (mot)

Div.Kartenstelle 190 (mot)

leichte Infanterie Rgt. 155 (mot) *

Stabskompanie (mot)

Infanterie Geschütz Kompanie 707 (sfl)

I.Bataillon (mot)

   Stab (mot)

      1.–4.Schützen Kp. (mot)

II.Bataillon (mot)

   Stab (mot)

      5.–8.Schützen Kp. (mot)

leichte Infanterie Rgt. 200 * **

Stabskompanie

Infanterie Geschütz Kompanie 708 (sfl)

I.Bataillon

   Stab

      1.–4.Schützen Kp.

II.Bataillon

   Stab

      5.–8.Schützen Kp.

leichte Infanterie Rgt. 361 * **

Stabskompanie

Infanterie Geschütz Kompanie (from August 1942?)

I.Bataillon

   Stab

      1.–4.Schützen Kp.

II.Bataillon

   Stab (mot)

      5.–8.Schützen Kp.

Artillerie Abteilung 361 (mot)

(on 20 August 1942 becomes I./Art.Rgt. 190 (mot))

Stab (mot)

Nachrichtenzug (mot)

1.–3.Batterie (mot)

1./613 Fla Kp. (mot) – (on 20 August 1942 becomes Flak Kp. 190 (mot))

Aufklärungs Abt. 580 (mot) §

Stab (mot)

1.Panzerspäh Komp. (mot)

2.leichte Schützen Späh Kompanie (mot)

3.schwere Kompanie (mot)

4.(Beute) Batterie (mot)

leichte Kolonne (mot)

Pionier Bataillon 900 (mot)

Stab (mot)

1.–2.Pionier Kompanie (mot)

leichte Kolonne (mot)

Panzerjäger Abt. 190 (mot) +

Stab (mot)

1.–2.Panzerjäger Komp. (mot)

Pz Nachrichten Kp. 190 (mot)

(from August 1942 2.Kp./Pz Nachr.Abt. 190 (mot))

Artillerie Regiment 190 (mot)

(Forming in Germany from May 1942, should have absorbed Art.Abt. 361)

Stabsbatterie (mot)

I.Abteilung (mot) [from: Art.Abt. 361]

   Stabsbatterie (mot)

      1.–3.Batterie (mot)

II.Abteilung (mot)

   Stabsbatterie (mot)

      4.–6.Batterie (mot)

Panzer Abteilung 190

(Forming in Germany from May 1942)

(continues on page 39)

Panzer Nachrichten Abteilung 190 (mot)

(Forming in Germany from May 1942, should have absorbed Pz Nachrichten Kp. 190 as its 2. Kompanie)

Feldersatz Bataillon 90/190

(Forming in Germany from May 1942, was temporarily replaced in July by a Marschbataillon. Since late August)

Attached from May 1942:

Panzerjäger Abt. 605 (sfl)

Stab (mot)

Nachrichtenzug (mot)

1.–3.Panzerjäger Komp. (sfl)

Fla Bataillon 606 (sfl)

Stab (mot)

1.–3.Fla Kompanie (sfl)

Sonderverband 288 (mot)

(organization as of 20 May 1942)

Stabskompanie (mot)

Aufklärungskompanie (mot)

I.Bataillon (mot)

   Stab (mot)

      1.–4.Kompanie (mot)

II.Bataillon

   Stab (mot)

      5.–8.Kompanie (mot)

Support units as of 15 August 1942:

Div.Nachschub Führer 190 (mot)

Stab (mot)

Kleine Kw Kolonne 1–4/190 (mot)

Werkstatt Komp. 190 (mot)

Nachschub Kp. 190

Divisions Verpflegungsamt 190

Schlachterei Kompanie 190

(Bäckerei Kompanie 190, added later)

Sanitäts Kompanie 288 (mot)

Krankenkraftwagenzug 2/592 (mot) (later 1–2/190)

Feldgendarmerietrupp 190 (mot)

Feldpostamt 190 (mot)

* *motorized from August 1942*
§ *officially formed on 20 May 1942 (already existed on 10 May)*
+ *1./Pz.Jäg. 190 from 1./Pz.Jäg.Abt. 33, 2./Pz.Jäg. 190 from 5./MG Batl. 8*
* ** *leichte Infanterie Regiment renamed Panzergrenadier Regiment on 26 July 1942 (subunits renamed accordingly) Both II./Artillerie Regiment 190 and Panzer Abteilung 190 landed in Tunisia in November 1944*
Notes:
- *Bäckerei Kp. 535/ Schlachterei Kp. 715/Krankenkraftwagen Zug 638 – temporarily attached after mid-April 1942. Divisions Verpflegungs Amt, Feldgendarmerie Trupp and Feldpostamt had to be attached as well.*
- *Divisions Nachschub Führer 90 and Nachschub Kompanie 90 were created in mid-May 1942. Furthermore, Sanitäts Staffel 288 (from Sonderverband 288) was attached.*
- *On 15 August 1942 divisional support units were renumbered from 90 to 190. These included: DiNaFü 190 (with: kleine Kraftwagenkolonne 1–4, mostly without vehicles, Werkstatt Kompanie 190, created from Werkstatt Zug 288, and Nachschub Kompanie 190), Schlachterei Kompanie 190, Divisions Verpflegungs Amt 190, Sanitäts Kompanie 288, Krankenkraftwagen Zug 2/592, Feldpostamt 190 and Feldgendarmerie Trupp 190 (a Bäckerei Kompanie 190 seems to have been forming). The only change in October 1942 is the appearance of Krankenkraftwagen Zug 1–2/190.*

eventually became 164.leichte Afrika Division on 1 September 1942 (**Fig 9**). In spite of the similarity of its designation to 90.leichte Afrika Division, it had a quite different organization (three infantry regiments each with three battalions) and, above all, lacked any *Panzerjäger* unit and any adequate degree of motorization (its established strength was about 13,000). With such a mixture of units, in which armour no longer played the dominant role, the Panzerarmee and DAK faced the long-awaited British offensive.

A German column moving in the desert at full speed. The first vehicle on the right is a Demag D7 SdKfz 10 towing a 37mm Pak 35/36, an anti-tank gun already obsolete by 1940, which was soon replaced by the 50mm Pak 38, though several were still used by infantry units as late as October 1942. (Carlo Pecchi Collection)

Table 9: 164.leichte Afrika Division, 1 September 1942

(Oberst Carl-Hans Lungershausen)

Stab (mot)

Div.Kartenstelle 220 (mot)

Nachrichten Kp. 220 (mot)

Panzergrenadier Rgt. 125

Stabskompanie

13.Infanterie Geschütz Kompanie

leichte Kolonne (mot)

I.Bataillon

    Stab

    1.–4.PzGren Kp.

II.Bataillon

    Stab

    5.–8.PzGren Kp.

III.Bataillon

    Stab

    9.–12.PzGren Kp.

Panzergrenadier Rgt. 382

Stabskompanie

13.Infanterie Geschütz Kompanie

leichte Kolonne (mot)

I.Bataillon

    Stab

    1.–4.PzGren Kp.

II.Bataillon

    Stab

    5.–8.PzGren Kp.

III.Bataillon

    Stab

    9.–12.PzGren Kp.

Panzergrenadier Rgt. 433

Stabskompanie

13.Infanterie Geschütz Kompanie

leichte Kolonne (mot)

I.Bataillon

    Stab

    1.–4.PzGren Kp.

II.Bataillon

    Stab

    5.–8.PzGren Kp.

III.Bataillon

    Stab

    9.–12.PzGren Kp.

Artillerie Regiment 220 (mot)

Stabsbatterie (mot)

I.Abteilung (mot)

    Stabsbatterie (mot)

    1.–3. Batterie (mot)

II.Abteilung (Gebirgsartillerie)

    Stabsbatterie

    4.–6. Batterie

Aufklärungs Abt. (mot) 220 *

Stab (mot)

1.Panzerspäh Komp. (mot)

2.leichte Schützen Späh Kompanie (mot)

3.schwere Kompanie (mot)

4.(Beute) Batterie (mot)

leichte Kolonne (mot)

Pionier Bataillon 220 (mot)

Stab (mot)

1.–3.Pionier Kompanie (mot)

leichte Kolonne (mot)

Div.Nachschub Führer 220 (mot)

Stab (mot)

Kleine Kw Kolonne 1–3/220 (mot)

Werkstatt Komp. 220

Nachschub Kp. 220

Divisions Verpflegungsamt 220

Schlachterei Kompanie 220

Bäckerei Kompanie 220

Sanitäts Kompanie 1–2/220

Krankenkraftwagenzug 1-2/220

Feldgendarmerietrupp 220 (mot)

Feldpostamt 220 (mot)

* forming

Fig. 9: 164.leichte Afrika Division, 1 September 1942

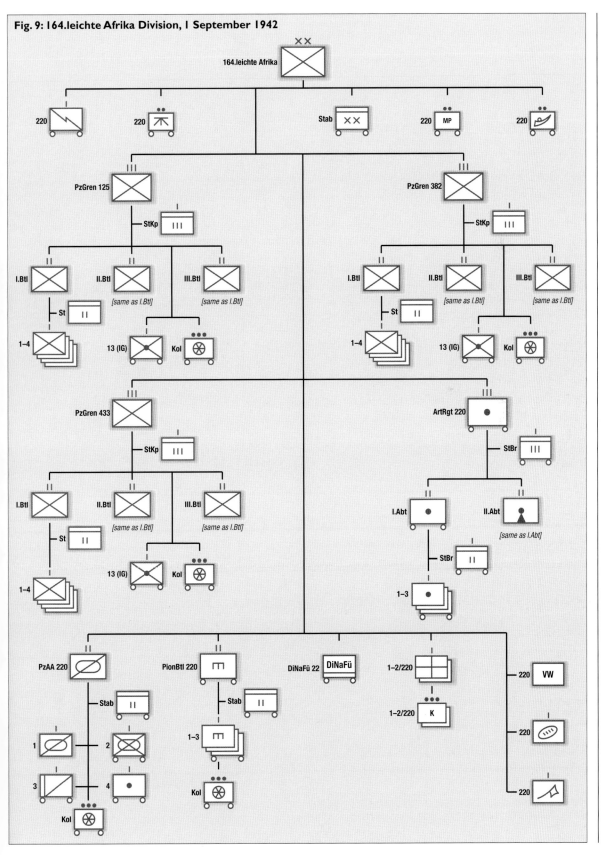

Tactics

Based on combined-arms warfare, unit coordination and flexibility, German armoured tactics in 1941 were advanced, but not always suitable for desert warfare. They had been developed for use in Europe, and in particular Western Europe, which is where the German Army was designed to fight. They had also been shaped by the campaigns in Poland and Western Europe in 1939–40. Terrain was a prime factor: these countries had many natural hurdles like rivers and mountains, and a more or less extensive road network. Therefore, attention was focused on the seizure of particular key points – bridges, towns with crossroads, high points – possession of which had tactical and operational importance. Since these points were often fortified and heavily defended by the enemy, tactics for use in attacks against the enemy's main line of resistance were given particular attention. German armoured tactics were therefore structured into three different phases: assault, breakout and exploitation. Divisional reconnaissance units took the lead by creating a reconnaissance screen with the task of reporting the presence and movement of enemy units. Once contact had been established and information had been obtained, the suitability of the terrain was checked and finally an area was chosen for the *Schwerpunkt*. The assault was then conducted with infantry, armour and support units acting in close cooperation under the cover of artillery fire and, when possible, air support. Once enemy defences had been broken through, mobile units advanced deep and fast with the aim of cutting off the enemy units from their communications and supply lines, while non-mobile units secured the area. Eventually, enemy forces were encircled and finally destroyed.

Some aspects of these tactics worked well in the Western Desert in spite of the completely different environment. Even though mobile, fast-advancing units proved effective during both the March–April 1941 and the January–February 1942 German drives into Cyrenaica, the same did not apply to the tactic of encircling enemy units. Because of the troubles experienced in attacking prepared positions, often defended by large minefields, the DAK took full advantage of the terrain and turned to fluid movement tactics. This enabled it to surround and attack enemy formations on their flanks and rear, though not

A Horch Kfz 16 medium staff car at a crossroads not far from Agedabia, actually almost halfway between Mersa el Brega and Benghazi (the roadsigns give the Italian names). Apart from the bone on the radiator, apparently a very common practice amongst DAK vehicles, the large 'K' on the right mudguard is noticeable. Apparently this is the insignia used by units belonging to Panzergruppe 1 von Kleist on the Eastern Front; this is also suggested by the two small letters above it (GR). (Carlo Pecchi Collection)

always successfully as the enemy often took advantage of the terrain: in many cases, their motorized units were able to escape the trap. The lack of key geographical features, so common in the European theatre of operations, rendered encirclement harder to obtain, but much was also owed to the lack of adequate training and knowledge of the terrain. During 1941, these factors prevented the Germans from effectively implementing their approach to battle. In many cases failure was due to the lack of the necessary battlefield experience and training of German units, which thus lacked the vital close cooperation and coordination required. One of the consequences was that, even when they prevailed on the battlefield, German units suffered heavy losses, eventually resulting in a strategic defeat given their numerical inferiority.

A noticeable gap was the inadequacy of German tank versus tank combat tactics. This key area of fighting had only been developed in late 1940 and early 1941; before that the Panzer forces been expected to avoid fighting enemy armour and focus on speed and manoeuvre. However, as experience in the Western Desert in 1941 had shown, manoeuvre alone could not defeat the enemy, and by then the German armoured forces suffered from their lack of training and experience. An ingenuous solution was found in the principles of combined-arms warfare, unit coordination and cooperation that had already been successfully used during the British *Brevity* and *Battleaxe* operations in the Sollum–Halfaya area. The idea adopted was to defeat enemy armour by using anti-tank guns in close cooperation with the infantry and the Panzers. Fully developed in early 1942, this tactic saw the Germans using a front-line screen of strongpoints made of anti-tank guns and infantry that, since the British forces also lacked adequate coordination and training in combined-arms warfare, could easily repulse enemy attacks whilst inflicting heavy casualties. Once this had been achieved the Panzers would intervene, attacking the badly mauled enemy units and using their speed and manoeuvrability to destroy them. This tactic was so successful that, from the late summer of 1942, the British Army began to retrain its armoured units to operate in a very similar way.

Ras el Mdauuar, 30 April–1 May 1941

After its successful advance into Cyrenaica, the DAK faced its first defeat during the assault on Tobruk. This was not just due solely to the lack of forces available, but was also the result of lack of training and of inadequate assault tactics. These tactics were actually based on a combination of fire and movement that, though successful in North-Western Europe, was likely to break down against a determined and stubborn defender. Selected assault areas were quite narrow, with each battalion being allotted a front between 400 and 1,000m wide. Infantry, Panzer and support units were supposed to work in close coordination under the cover of a short and violent artillery barrage. The assault itself could be carried out in two different ways: infantry either infiltrated the enemy defences or performed a direct assault under cover of Panzer and heavy weapon fire. Fire itself was aimed against selected targets (enemy's anti-tank guns, machine-gun and heavy weapons' nests); there was also area fire, used to pin down enemy troops. Infantry led the attack with the task of seizing and securing enemy positions, thus allowing tanks, support units and follow-up waves of infantry to advance. These moved into the target area as soon as the enemy's anti-tank and heavy guns had been silenced starting a new phase of the attack, which was now split into two separate elements. Follow-up units, supported by machine guns and anti-tank guns, secured the area and prepared to meet any possible counterattack while the leading infantry units pressed on, deeply penetrating the enemy position; at the same time tanks broke out to target headquarters, field maintenance centres and supply depots to spread panic and confusion. To assure a deep penetration commanders were urged not to worry unduly about their flanks, supposedly protected by the advancing infantry and follow-up units, whose tasks also included the mopping-up of the whole area.

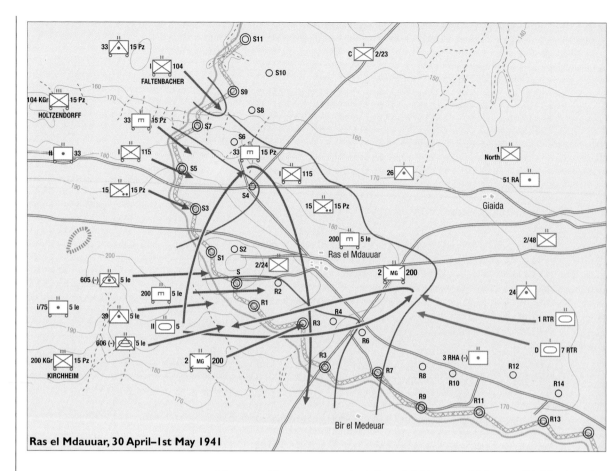

Ras el Mdauuar, 30 April–1st May 1941

Many problems were met at Ras el Mdauuar; 15.Panzer Division's units, grouped under Kampfgruppe Holtzendorff (from Stab Schützen Regiment 104), had just arrived in Africa and were rather inexperienced. Also its commander, like the commander of Kampfgruppe Kirchheim (from Regiments Stab zbV 200), had only recently joined his unit. The latter, however, proved wiser since he decided to ignore Rommel's order to avoid any terrain reconnaissance in order not to alert the enemy; a useless precaution since the Australians detected German movements as soon as they started. In the end, lack of proper training for night fighting prevented the Germans from seizing the strongpoints around Ras el Mdauuar, thus leaving a gap between the two assault groups. The battle was hard fought by both sides and on the morning of 1 May the Germans renewed their assault by bringing forward II./Panzer Regiment 5. Its task was to support the advance of Pionier Bataillon 200 and of MG Bataillon 2 south of the crossroads, to which task it committed most of its tanks: nine PzKpfw I, 26 PzKpfw II, 36 PzKpfw III and 8 PzKpfw IV – all the running tanks of the regiment. What should have been a decisive move ended in failure; the Panzers advanced but soon lost contact with the infantry units they were supposed to support, and that had already been shown to lack coordination skills. During their advance the Panzers fell prey to the anti-tank guns of 24th and 26th Australian Brigades, which were firing well beyond German infantry weapons' range, before eventually running into a minefield. All in all, 14 tanks were lost. At 0900hrs Rommel recalled the assault forces and the Panzers went over to the defensive while infantry secured the area. An Australian counterattack came in the afternoon, led by the Matildas of 7th RTR and the Crusaders of 1st RTR. It was now their turn to face a crossfire when the Panzers attacked them from three sides; they lost four Matildas and two Cruisers before withdrawing.

Two days of battle – Sidi Rezegh, 22–23 November 1941

In 1941, the DAK showed better cooperation and coordination skills in defence than in attack, as is demonstrated by its failures against Tobruk and by its successes at Sollum and Halfaya. However, Operation *Crusader* offered the first real occasion to fight a battle in the open in which the German tactics proved once more superior to the British ones. Following a slow initial reaction, four days after the British attack the DAK struck back. One of the first major blows was delivered on 22 November when Panzer Regiment 8, moving north to establish contact with Afrika Regiment 361 on the ridge below Sidi Muftah, encountered the 8th Hussars still deployed in its night leaguer along with the HQ of the 4th Armoured Brigade.

The Panzer attack formation adopted here is quite typical and worth being described in detail; it was known as a 'wide wedge' (*Breitkeil*) and was based on an inverted triangle of three *Panzer Kompanien*, with the two light ones deployed forward. This formation offered the advantage of a large number of guns forward while still holding a suitable proportion in reserve. When necessary, this formation could also break into a three-pronged attack.

At dusk the forward elements of I./Panzer Regiment 8 (mostly from the leichte Panzerzug) entered the night leaguer of 4th Armoured Brigade to the surprise of both parties. The Germans reacted first and the three advancing companies opened fire on the British tanks, which were light M3 Honeys.

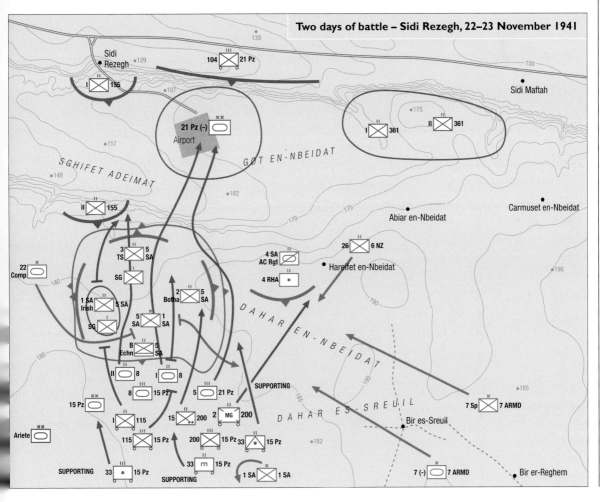

Two days of battle – Sidi Rezegh, 22–23 November 1941

45

Rommel talking with Italian officers in the summer of 1941. Relations with the Italians were never easy, nor was cooperation in the field. On many occasions Rommel blamed Italian troops (in particular their officers) for having not carried out his orders. The Italians, on the other hand, claimed he was only looking for a convenient scapegoat. (Archivio Ufficio Storico Stato Maggiore Esercito)

Hammered by German fire, some of the British tanks were destroyed and others set on fire, which then provided the illumination that the German gunners required to finish their job. Three hours later the 8th Hussars had been wiped out: 35 tanks and many other weapons and vehicles had been destroyed or captured, along with one brigadier, 17 officers and 150 other ranks.

When enemy formations were encountered in the open field, the Germans fell back on the meeting-engagement tactic (*Begegnungsgefecht*), based on a combination of a frontal attack, to provoke an enemy reaction, and a flank attack, aimed at delivering a fatal blow to the enemy's less defended areas. Unit coordination was therefore essential, which is what the Germans failed to obtain on 23 November. On *Totensonntag*, the Sunday of the dead, the reinforced 15.Panzer Division (with Panzer Regiment 5 attached) moved against the 5th South African Brigade that was leaguered south of Point 176, threatening Sidi Rezegh's airfield and pass. Once more, the German attack tactics were typical; the main thrust was led by Panzer Regiment 8 on the left and Panzer Regiment 5 on the right flank, both closely supported by advance artillery units. Behind them came the infantry, Schützen Regiment 115 behind Panzer Regiment 8 and Regiment 200 behind Panzer Regiment 5, the latter supported by Panzerjäger Abteilung 33 and Panzer Pionier Bataillon 33, while the bulk of the divisional artillery supported the two advancing prongs. The scheme was that of a classical *Begegnungsgefecht*, with Panzer Regiment 8 and Schützen Regiment 115 leading a frontal attack against the enemy while Panzer Regiment 5 and Regiment 200 attacked its left wing. The Italian Ariete armoured division was to protect 15.Panzer Division's left flank, though not much was expected from it and actually no support came at all. The events of *Totensonntag* clearly show that the tactics actually worked, but also that the DAK still needed to improve its unit coordination and training. After an intense artillery bombardment the attack began, soon turning into chaos. I./Panzer Regiment 8 moved north through the brigade trains position, soon losing contact with Schützen Regiment 115. To its left, II./Panzer Regiment 8 attacked the 1st South African Irish Regiment to allow I./Schützen Regiment 115 to advance, only to face the counterattack led by 22nd Brigade's Composite Regiment. On the other flank, Panzer Regiment 5's sluggish movement prevented it from taking part in the attack and it eventually moved north to rejoin the rest of the division at Sidi Rezegh. In fact, the right prong simply vanished: only Kradschützen Bataillon 15 attacked 2nd Botha's positions, while MG Bataillon 2 and part of Panzerjäger Abteilung 33 faced a possible threat on their right and also 22nd Armoured Brigade's counterattack.

DAK's charge against 5th South African Brigade was therefore carried out mostly by Panzer Regiment 8 and Schützen Regiment 115, which closely followed the Panzers with its truck-borne infantry. Fierce South African resistance soon caused the attack to break into a series of small, hard clashes that disintegrated the cohesion and coordination of the German units. Infantry lost contact with the armour, sometimes moving even ahead of them, and I./Schützen Regiment 115 actually reached Point 176 alone. Even the two *Panzer Abteilungen* took a different course, with I./Panzer Regiment 8 advancing north to Sidi Rezegh's airfield, leaving II./Panzer Regiment 8 behind to face a counterattack from 22nd Armoured Brigade, which was eventually repulsed by 1./Panzerjäger Abteilung 33. By nightfall 5th South African Brigade had been almost completely wiped out, though at a very high price. On 23 November Panzer Regiment 8 alone suffered the following losses: 14 out of 32 PzKpfw II (six permanently), 30 out of 68 PzKpfw III (ten permanently) and nine out of 16 PzKpfw IV (three permanently).

Belhamed, 1–2 December 1941

A key German tactical obsession was the need to control high ground, essential for dominating surrounding areas and allowing accurate pinpointing of enemy forces for artillery fire. In the last days of November 1941, after the unsuccessful 'dash to the wire', the DAK attempted to cut the corridor that the 2nd New Zealand Division had established with the Tobruk garrison. Here, combat focused on the two vital heights to the north and north-west of Sidi Rezegh: Ed Duda and Belhamed. By 1 December only the latter was still in New Zealanders' hands, a last link with the Tobruk perimeter, and the Germans considered control of the point vital to cut that link. Once more the attack was led by the tanks of Panzer Regiment 8 (with about 40 AFVs remaining) supported by infantry from MG Bataillon 2 and Kradschützen Bataillon 15, with covering fire provided by Artillerie Regiment 33. The approach used on this occasion was an improvement over the standard German assault tactics: Panzers and infantry approached and attacked their target separately to avoid being caught together under enemy artillery fire. Improved coordination led to success in what was described as one of Panzer Regiment 8's hardest battles. The assault against the Belhamed positions, held by two battalions of the 4th New Zealand Brigade supported by artillery and anti-tank guns, started at 0630hrs on 1 December. It took one and half an hours to break the enemy defences and, after two more hours, the heights were secured. The situation was still fluid, however, since, while the New Zealanders' retreated to Zaafran, 4th Armoured Brigade (with 115 tanks, the remnants of 7th Armoured Division) attacked from the south through the positions still held by 6th New Zealand Brigade. Accurate artillery fire from Artillerie Regiment 33 and the immediate redeploying of 12 Panzers from I./Panzer Regiment 8 to form an anti-tank screen soon halted the attack. The Germans had now the chance to continue their own offensive.

Unfortunately, after almost two weeks of battle, DAK's combat strength was at its lowest ebb and there were not enough men to surround the New Zealanders forces. While Panzer Regiment 8 and the supporting MG Bataillon 2 and Kradschützen Bataillon 15 continued their attack toward Zaafran, 21.Panzer Division attacked to the west in an attempt to cut off the retreating New Zealanders. Marching along the Trigh Capuzzo some infantry reached Sidi Rezegh to find it already in German hands, but the 21 tanks remaining in Panzer Regiment 5 proved too few to support II./SR 104's advance toward Bir Sciuerat. On 2 December the New Zealanders decided to abandon Zaafran and, pressed by 15.Panzer Division's attacks from the west, they withdrew at dusk to the east, eventually joining the 7th Armoured Division south of Tobruk. The Germans secured the heights and re-established a perimeter around Tobruk, but the enemy had suffered no major loss and could attack again – something the DAK could no longer do. Three days later Rommel ordered Axis forces to withdraw west of Tobruk, the first step in their retreat.

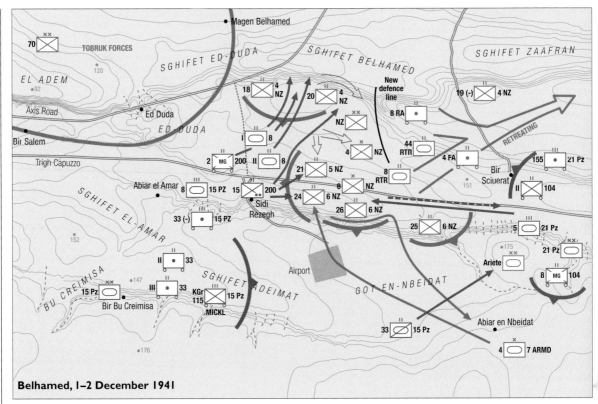

Belhamed, 1–2 December 1941

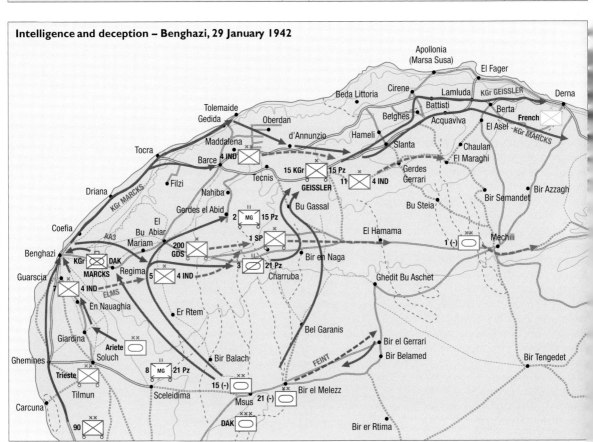

Intelligence and deception – Benghazi, 29 January 1942

Intelligence and deception – Benghazi, 29 January 1942

Rommel's second drive into Cyrenaica was an even greater success than that of 1941. At the beginning it had actually been more frustrating as greater numbers of British troops had been able to escape the German trap at Agedabia and, a week after the drive had started on 22 January, the outcome was in the balance due to the precarious supply system and the weakness of the Axis forces, Mussolini asked Rommel not to advance deeply into Cyrenaica and instead to establish a defensive line west of Agedabia. Rommel ignored him and DAK's mobile forces proceeded with their advance until they reached Msus on 25 January. Again, British forces avoided destruction and succeeded in withdrawing to the line Benghazi–El Abiar–Charruba. While still waiting for Italian mobile forces to arrive, Rommel faced an apparently troublesome situation. In spite of their heavy losses (including about 300 AFVs), British troops still held northern Cyrenaica, whilst there were also two retreating Indian brigades still to the south-west of Msus. However, Romel had a very good idea about the disposition and capability of the British forces and that very same day Panzerarmee Afrika's command formed the opinion there was no large enemy formations in Cyrenaica capable of counterattacking in the short term. Also, one of the 26th Panzerarmee's intelligence officers, Major Friedrich von Mellenthin, reported that on the basis of signal intelligence most of the British units had withdrawn north of the line El Abiar–Charruba. Intelligence also revealed that British commanders were completely uncertain about their own defensive strategy. In conclusion Mellenthin could say that an evacuation of Benghazi was not excluded and that the British commanders expected the DAK to attack toward Mechili, thus getting round the Djebel Achdar, the green mountains. Rommel had attacked this way before – as had Wavell and Auchinleck for the British – but this time he had another plan.

Logistics played a significant part in his decision: DAK's supply bases were still close to El Agheila, where the offensive had started, and a long advance would have imposed too severe a strain on the already strained supply lines. Rommel decided instead to go for a sudden attack against Benghazi under his own personal command, while the bulk of the DAK was to make a feint attack toward Mechili and prepare to continue its advance further. On the other side of the hill, 25 January was also a fateful day. XIII Corps commander, General Godwin-Austen, ordered the 4th Indian Division to withdraw from Benghazi and the 1st Armoured Division to move to Mechili, but General Neil Ritchie, temporary commander of Eighth Army, eventually cancelled these orders as he still thought a British counterattack was possible. He then ordered the 4th

A mixed Panzer column on the move. From left to right are a PzKpfw II, a PzKpfw IV and two PzKpfw III. Such a mixture was quite unusual since PzKpfw III and IV did not belong to the same *Panzerkompanie*. (Carlo Pecchi Collection)

A German medical column (note the red cross on the lorry's left mudguard) negotiates Tobruk's anti-tank ditch on a makeshift bridge. *Pionier* units left their bridging columns back in Germany due to the difficulties of transportation. (Carlo Pecchi Collection)

Indian Division to hold Benghazi and, given the DAK's presence at Msus, ordered the 1st Armoured Division to defend Mechili. Having prepared themselves between 26 and 28 January, the attack started on the 29th with Kampfgruppe Marcks (composed of Stab and II./Schützen Regiment 104, I.–II./SR 115, Panzerjäger Abteilung 605 and a *Flak Batterie*), reinforced with elements from both Aufklärungs Abteilungen 3 and 33, moved against Benghazi under cover of the DAK's feint toward Mechili. This successfully distracted the British commanders while, undetected, KGr Marcks reached and eventually seized Benghazi, destroying part of 7th Indian Brigade and capturing a large amount of booty.

A wise use of intelligence and deception had granted Rommel his coveted success and, on 30 January, he was promoted to the rank of *Generaloberst*. He celebrated this promotion with the launch of a new, daring offensive that eventually regained him the whole of western Cyrenaica. With the bulk of his troops still lying in the Msus–Benghazi area, Rommel attacked along the coastal road using KGr Marcks, while KGr Geissler (formed around 15.Schützen Brigade with the bulk of Regiments Stab zbV 200) and Aufklärungs Abteilung 3 advanced throughout the Djabel Achdar toward Maraua. At this point Ritchie ordered a general withdraw of Eighth Army and British troops abandoned western Cyrenaica, falling back to the Gazala–Bir Hacheim line. By 3 February the two advancing German columns, now moving almost together, were beyond Derna. Three days later Rommel's second drive into Cyrenaica halted at the Gazala Line, putting an end to another successful use of fast-moving columns.

Flächenmarsch at Gazala, 26 May 1942

The German plan for Operation *Theseus* was, at first glance, extremely simple and straightforward. A closer look reveals how complicated and daring it actually was. The British defensive line at Gazala had many Achilles' heels. Built to defend the main Libyan road (Via Balbia) and Tobruk, the Gazala–Bir Hacheim Line was part of a large defensive system based on a series of strongpoints built around extensive minefields known as 'boxes', manned by infantry, which became 'fortresses without walls'. Its biggest flaw was the fact that it only extended for about 60km from the coast, hence it could be outflanked by enemy motorized formations. Of course Eighth Army's command considered such a possibility and took precautions, mostly in the form of large concentrations of armoured and motorized units to the south-east of the line,

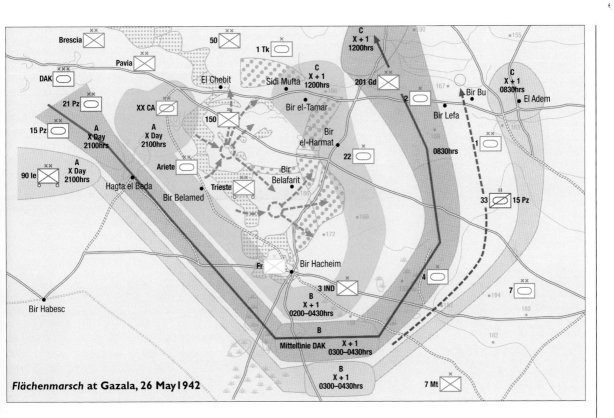

Flächenmarsch at Gazala, 26 May 1942

Map labels:
Brescia — 50 — 1 Tk — C X + 1 1200hrs
Pavia — El Chebit — Sidi Mufta — C X + 1 1200hrs — 201 Gd — C X + 1 0830hrs — El Adem
DAK — Bir el-Tamar — Bir Bu
21 Pz — XX CA — 2 — Bir Lefa
150 — Bir el-Harmat — 0830hrs — 1
15 Pz — A X Day 2100hrs — A X Day 2100hrs — 22
90 le — A X Day 2100hrs — Ariete — Bir Belafarit — 33 — 15 Pz
Hagta el Beda — Trieste
Bir Belamed
Fr — Bir Hacheim — 4
3 IND — 7
B X + 1 0200–0430hrs
Bir Habesc — B Mittellinie DAK — X + 1 0300–0430hrs
B X + 1 0300–0430hrs — 7 Mt

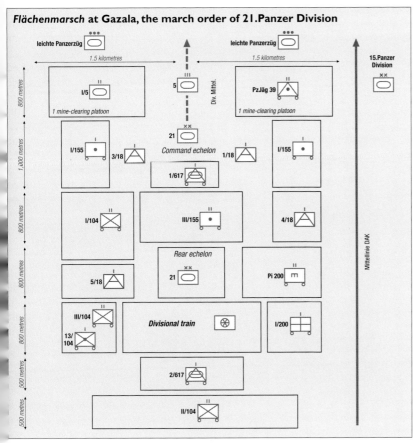

Flächenmarsch at Gazala, the march order of 21.Panzer Division

leichte Panzerzüg — leichte Panzerzüg — 15.Panzer Division
1.5 kilometres — 1.5 kilometres
I/5 — 5 — PzJäg 39
1 mine-clearing platoon — Div. Mittel. — 1 mine-clearing platoon
I/155 — 3/18 — 21 — Command echelon — 1/18 — I/155
1/617
I/104 — III/155 — 4/18
Rear echelon
5/18 — 21 — Pi 200
III/104 — Divisional train — I/200
13/104
2/617
II/104
Mittellinie DAK
800 metres — 1,000 metres — 800 metres — 800 metres — 800 metres — 500 metres — 500 metres

TOP

The advance of Axis troops in the first stages of Operation *Theseus* had been carefully planned; 90.leichte Division was to cover the right flank of the DAK and advance to El Adem, along with Panzer Aufklärungs Abteilung 33, which was to fill the gap between 90.leichte and 15.Panzer Division. The main advance was in the centre, along DAK's 'middle line' of advance (Mittellinie). To its right was 15.Panzer Division, to its left 21.Panzer Division. The Italian XXI Corpo d'Armata was to move close to the British defences in order to break gaps in the minefields.

ready to face and counterattack any approaching enemy units. These units were a serious hurdle for any attacker, especially when some basic facts about desert warfare are taken into consideration. Unlike the European theatre of operations, the Western Desert possessed certain peculiarities that any commander had to take into account when preparing his plans. Firstly, it was practically impossible for any unit, especially a motorized one, to approach an enemy's position undetected during daylight. Large masses of men and vehicles were easy to see and their movement raised large clouds of dust that could be easily spotted. Also, moving by night was extremely hard since, in a featureless terrain like the desert, units had many problems locating their position during daylight let alone at night. Generally speaking, when darkness fell units on both sides 'leaguered' to get some rest and to give the supply column a chance to catch up.

This gave the defenders certain advantages. Had the Axis forces attempted to break through the line, the 'boxes' would have slowed them down enough to bring in reinforcements and gain local superiority. On the other hand, had they attempted to outflank the line, their movement would have been noticed and an armoured force would have quickly faced them. However, Rommel took a new approach and decided on a night attack. That would have been impossible just one year before, when the DAK was neither properly trained nor used to night combat, especially over unfamiliar terrain. Experience and training had made it possible, and Rommel's 'hook' around Gazala was based on a night march that involved more than four divisions, moving at first south to south-east, then turning east and finally to the north to north-east. The three groups, which consisted of the Italian XX Corpo d'Armata (with the motorized Trieste and armoured Ariete divisions) and the DAK (with 21. and 15.Panzer Divisions) and 90.leichte Infanterie Division had to reach their assembly areas after moving at dusk for about 40km. Then, at 2100hrs on X-Day, they were to start their advance and march almost parallel to the British minefields to reach their assembly areas south of Bir Hacheim ('B'). DAK alone had to cover about 50km in six or seven hours of darkness. Then, the three groups were to move from the 'B' position at dawn (0430hrs) on Day X+1, which is when the assault was scheduled to start. The next step was an advance to the north-east in which the DAK alone had to reach a mid-start line 40km away in less than four hours. Then it had to move north to north-west for another 20km until the final assembly point south of Acroma was reached by noon on Day X+1. All in all, the march was 110km in 15 hours, with more than a third at night. Considering that the DAK had orders to engage and destroy any enemy unit it encountered during the march, the progress it had made during the previous months is all too evident

It is worth noting that both Panzer divisions reverted to a tactic Rommel had already used with success in France in 1940. This was the *Flächenmarsch*, or 'area march'. It was based on marching with a wide front, with the units

Combined-arms warfare illustrated in a single image. A 1-ton Demag D7 SdKfz 10 towing a 37mm Pak 35/36 is moving close to a PzKpfw III Ausf. G, probably of Panzer Regiment 5 (note the white turret numbers). Given the appearance of the soldiers, the photo must have been taken in autumn 1941. (Carlo Pecchi Collection)

deployed in a way that would have enabled them to quickly react against any possible threat. Deployed in the shape of a wide rectangle, at least 3km wide and 5.2km deep, 21.Panzer Division advanced using a typical marching formation: Panzer and Panzerjäger units led the way closely followed by the divisional artillery and anti-aircraft units, accompanied by an infantry battalion. Other infantry units, along with the divisional trains and medical services under cover of a single *Fla Kompanie*, marched at the rear ready to move forward or cover the flanks. Considering how close units were to each other, moving those large columns required great management and skill, especially at night. Although the original plan eventually failed, the DAK carried out the march as requested and finally won the battle.

El Mreir, 21–22 July 1942

According to German defensive tactics, a defence line was established in depth with the aim of exhausting the enemy's attacking forces; the defenders were to hold their positions without caring about enemy penetrations. At the same time reserves were to counterattack with the aim of destroying any enemy breakthrough. Anti-tank guns played a major role in the defence, as did the Panzers, whose role was to carry out immediate counterattacks. The principle of *Schild und Schwert* (shield and sword) ruled DAK tactics after Operations *Brevity* and *Battleaxe*, and it shaped the armoured warfare tactics that were successfully used at Gazala. Only a year later, at El Alamein, did these tactics break down under extreme conditions. In early July, after some one and a half months of fighting from Gazala to Alamein, the DAK and Axis forces in North Africa had suffered heavy losses and a corresponding fall in morale. The Italians eventually broke down and the advance toward Suez was halted. Reinforcements began to arrive, but the crisis was not yet over and British counterattacks now started. These focused in the area of Ruwesait that, by mid-July, was defended by both 21. and 15.Panzer Divisions, both with less than one-third of their established combat strengths. The British forces, on the other hand, included fresh and up-to-strength units. The newly arrived 23rd Armoured Brigade contained about 150 tanks in mid-July, mostly Valentines along with some Matildas. Both Panzer Regiment 5 and 8 only had six PzKpfw II, 33 PzKpfw III (six of which were 'special') and three PzKpfw IV (two of which were 'special'). Eighth Army HQ ordered an assault against the ridges of Deir el Shein, Deir el Abyad and El Mreir for 21 July with the aim of breaking through the DAK defence lines.

The assault started by nightfall after a strong artillery bombardment. In the north, 5th Indian Brigade attacked positions held by the Italians and III./Schützen Regiment 104 at Deir el Shein–Ruwesait, though without much success. The following morning at 0800hrs reserves were brought up and a gap was produced in the German defences. In the south the 6th New Zealand Brigade attacked through the positions held by the III./Schützen Regiment 115 and II./Schützen Regiment 104 with no better fortune, though they managed to reach the El Mreir depression. Daybreak on 22 July was quite disappointing for the British as no major breakthrough had been obtained and British sappers had only opened a few lanes through the minefields in front of El Mreir. With the German infantry still holding its positions, the two Panzer regiments prepared to counterattack. Heavy artillery fire and British air supremacy had spread havoc and confusion amongst the defenders; communications were interrupted, and reports on the situation were lacking. Yet German command reacted quickly, helped by the fact that their infantry was holding its positions in spite of the enemy advance, which, in some cases, had almost surrounded them. By midnight on 21 July the DAK commander, Generalleutnant Walther K. Nehring, ordered both Panzer Regiments 5 and 8 to join together and attack at dawn to restore the situation; I./Schützen Regiment 104 was to support the attack. Both Panzer regiments set off for the assault during the night, something that particularly surprised the British and illustrates the skills of 21.Panzer Division's

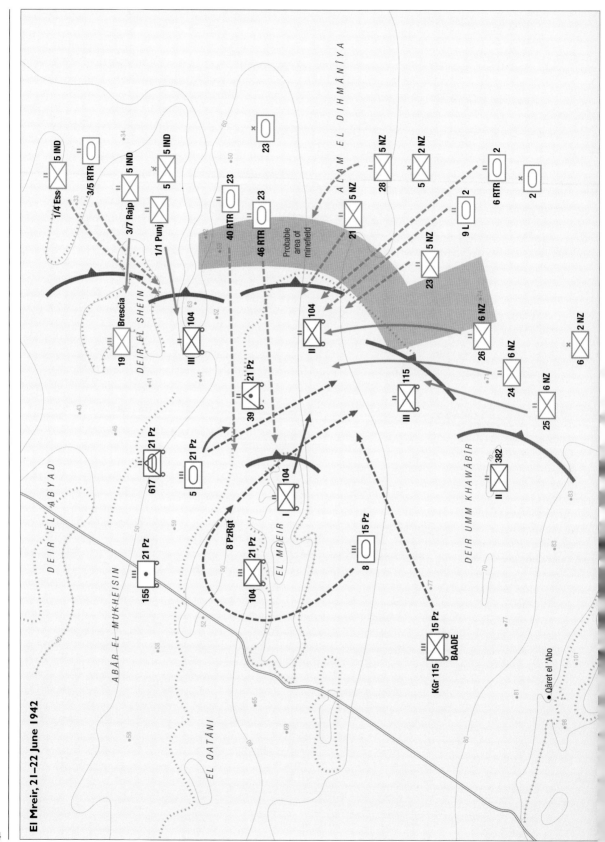

El Mreir, 21–22 June 1942

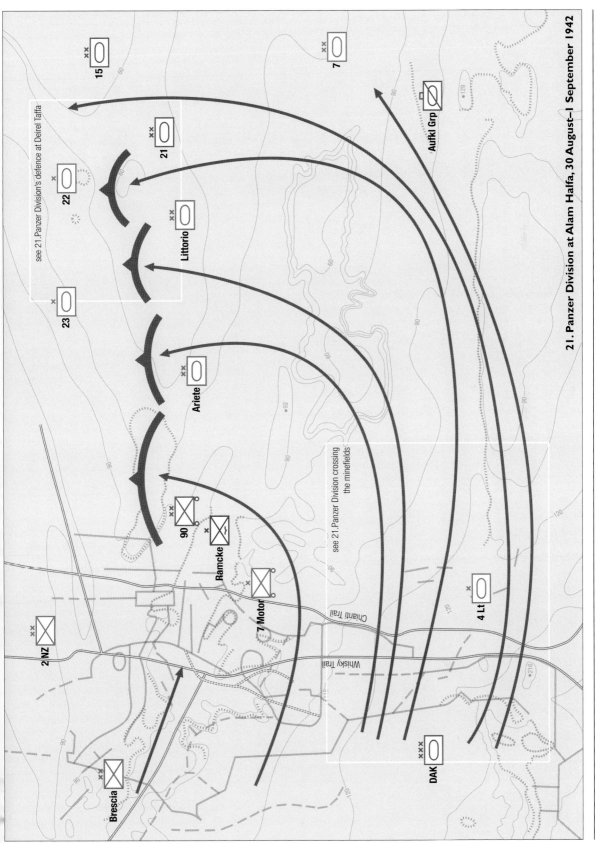

21. Panzer Division at Alam Halfa, 30 August–1 September 1942

15

7

see 21.Panzer Division's defence at Deir el Taffa

21

22

Littorio

23

Ariete

Aufkl Grp

90

Ramcke

7 Motor

2 NZ

Brescia

see 21.Panzer Division crossing the minefields

4 Lt

Chianti Trail

Whisky Trail

DAK

A 3-ton half-tracked Hanomag H kl 6 SdKfz 11 tractor speeding on a desert track. On its right mudguard can be barely distinguished the tactical symbol of a *Batterie leichte Feldhaubitze* (105mm), denoting it was serving with an artillery unit like Artillerie Regiment 155 or 33. (Carlo Pecchi Collection)

commander, Generalleutnant Georg von Bismarck. However, on the morning of 22 July the New Zealand infantry and British armour renewed their efforts. As expected, 23rd Armoured Brigade attacked through the minefields and, though it lost 17 tanks to mines and German fire, it reached its objective. 2nd Armoured Brigade was not so successful and its attempts to break through the minefields ended in a failure with the loss of 21 tanks. The German counterattack fell on already worn-out units; Panzer Regiments 5 and 8 moved against the positions held by the 23rd Armoured and the 6th New Zealand Brigade, now almost completely exposed on the El Mreir depression and already depleted by the losses inflicted by German defences. In a two-hour battle both British units suffered heavy casualties: 23rd Armoured Brigade lost about 40 tanks destroyed and 47 more damaged – about two-thirds of its strength – while 6th New Zealand Brigade lost about 700 men. The British attack was called off and the units withdrew, as did the Germans after a brief attempt to exploit their success.

Supply – 21.Panzer Division at Alam Halfa, 30 August 1942

Bringing supplies across the Mediterranean was only part of the Axis' logistical problem, since those supplies then had to be carried from harbours to the front and had to reach every division and unit. Only motorized columns could accomplish that, though they were extremely exposed to British air attacks, especially in the summer of 1942. Estimating divisional needs is quite hard, but an acceptable figure is no less than 300–400 tons (water excluded) for a Panzer division. The amount was mainly made up of ammunitions (about 100–200 tons) and petrol, oil and lubricants (POL, *c.*150 tons). The rest consisted of food, spare parts for vehicles and weapons, medical supplies and every other kind of supply needed by men and machines. Consumption of ammunition was extremely high when divisions were in combat, and stocks could be exhausted in a few days. For example, between 28 and 30 May 1942 21.Panzer Division consumed about 2,300 artillery rounds, 1,900 tank-gun rounds, 600 rounds for the 88mm guns and 340 more rounds for the 50mm anti-tank guns. During the ten days of the last Alamein battle, the division consumed about 10,000 tank-gun rounds and 12,000 artillery rounds, plus some 80,000 litres of water and 260,000 litres of fuel. Fuel was a major problem, especially because transport columns also burned it while moving from depots to the front line. In 1941 Panzer Regiment 5 needed as much as 4,400 litres of fuel for a single day of combat, about one-third of the fuel needed by all combat units (between 10,000 and 12,000 litres). Services and supply units included, the daily consumption of the entire division was about 33,000 litres. Water consumption too was extremely high, given the daily allowance of 3 litres per man in mid-1942 – vehicle-cooling water included. This figure had already been reduced from the daily allowance in 1941 of 5 litres per man.

Though often regarded as a kind of 'warriors' nightmare', logistics played a major role in the Western Desert, where everything had to be brought in across the sea and then straight to the front line. Its importance is clearly shown by 21.Panzer Division's experience during the last German offensive that eventually stopped at Alam Halfa. Problems had already been encountered while crossing the minefields, which were deeper than expected. Also, while trying to reach their objectives, units ran into a sandstorm that slowed down the pace of the advance and increased fuel consumption. Eventually, in the late afternoon of 30 August, 21.Panzer Division halted its march and deployed for defence. Logistics had won the battle over the warriors.

Defeat – 15.Panzer Division at El Alamein, 2 November 1942

There are various reasons behind the German defeat at El Alamein, and not all of them are obvious. British forces possessed an overwhelming superiority in numbers, though in the past months the DAK had defeated stronger enemies even when attacking. Lack of supplies was another reason, though this problem continuously plagued German forces in North Africa. Though those two reasons were important, the fact remains that the DAK was fighting a battle it could not win: a battle of attrition. The basic concept behind manoeuvre warfare was that while it enabled one to spare one's own forces, it also enabled one to wear down the enemy ones. Since German resources (and the Axis' ones in general) were inferior to those of their enemies, this was the only feasible way to wage war. North Africa offers a good example: as soon as the Germans had to give up movement warfare and turned to the hated *Stellungskrieg*, they simply surrendered their capability to inflict losses on the enemy while sparing their own forces. Their tactics and skill again proved superior, though not to the same extent as before, but they could not avoid defeat in the end. One, two or three enemy attacks could be repulsed and heavy losses could be inflicted on the attacker, but in the end the enemy's overwhelming superiority would impose itself.

During the first phase of the third Alamein battle, Operation *Lightfoot*, the British XXX Corps slowly made its way across the minefield boxes that faced the Axis lines. During this period, lasting between 23 and 28 October 1942, 15.Panzer Division was engaged according to German defensive tactics, which consisted of a series of counterattacks against enemy breakthroughs. It eventually won a tactical advantage since XXX Corps' advance was limited and no real breakthrough ever occurred, but it paid a very high cost: losses included about 220 tanks and armoured vehicles destroyed. In the meantime, however, XXX Corps gained a suitable starting line for its next assault, while 15.Panzer Division had lost most of its tanks and anti-tank weapons: by 28 October Panzer Regiment 8 was left with only 24 tanks, while Panzerjäger Abteilung 33 only had eight 50mm and one 76.2mm guns. Thus, when on 2 November Montgomery launched Operation *Supercharge* using available reserves, the German units facing it had been reduced to phantoms. They counterattacked nevertheless, and heavy losses were inflicted on the 9th Armoured Brigade. But as the day faded away, they faced a gloomy situation: Panzer Regiment 8 was left with eight tanks and the entire division was left with only six 50mm anti-tank guns, while about half of Panzergrenadier Regiment 115 had been annihilated. As Rommel knew well, when facing an enemy still capable of using its reserves there was no other option than retreat.

(For further details see *Campaign 158: El Alamein 1942* by Ken Ford, Osprey Publishing Ltd: Oxford, 2005.)

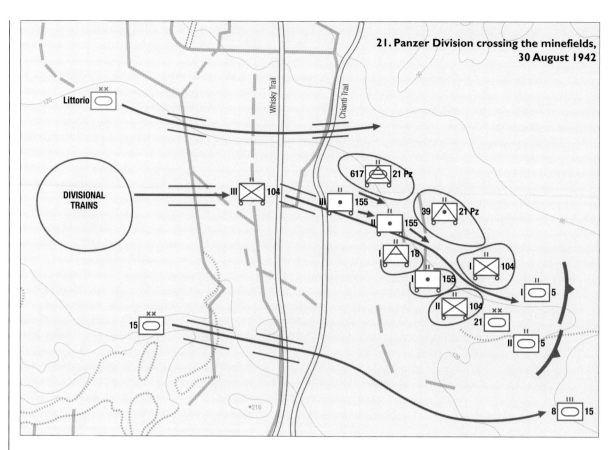

21. Panzer Division crossing the minefields, 30 August 1942

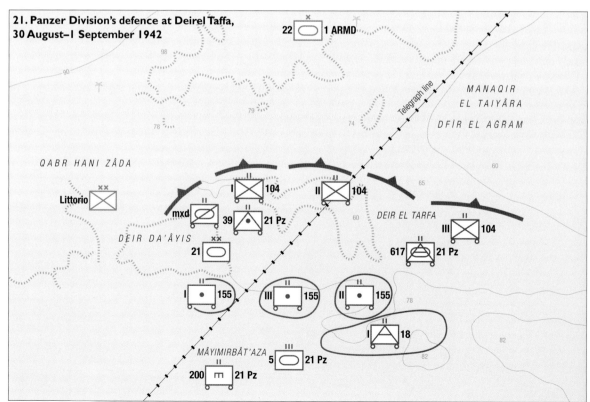

21. Panzer Division's defence at Deir el Taffa, 30 August–1 September 1942

58

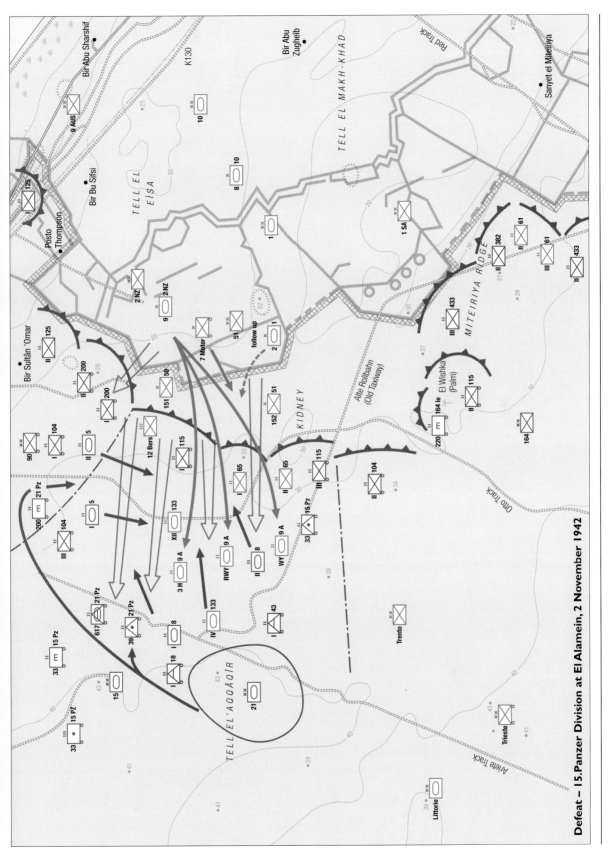

Defeat – 15.Panzer Division at El Alamein, 2 November 1942

Weapons and equipment

Two *Panzermänner* having a meal on top of their PzKpfw II tank. Food was always a major problem for DAK soldiers, in particular those supplied by the Italians. The tin can held by the soldier on right could be the infamous Italian 'AM' (for Amministrazione Militare, roughly equivalent to British War Department) canned meat soon renamed by the Germans *Alte Mann*, dead man. (Carlo Pecchi Collection)

German lack of preparedness to fight a war in the desert influenced the DAK's choice of weapons and equipment. Amongst the many problems encountered because of climate and environment, the suitability of their tropical uniforms had a particular effect on the German soldiers (for further details see *Elite 34: Afrikakorps 1941–43* by Gordon Williamson, Osprey Publishing Ltd: Oxford, 1991). Following their experiences in World War I in the German colonies, these uniforms were largely unsuitable for the Western Desert and quite uncomfortable for the soldiers. Unlike the British woollen uniforms, the German ones were made of cotton that made them cold at night and warm during the day, while their dark colour soon faded and the material absorbed the morning mist, making them unbearable. The jackets were uncomfortable (those who could used borrowed Italian sahariana jackets) and trousers, especially shorts, were quite impractical. The German tropical helmet was also soon discarded in favour of the steel one, the only one of any practical use in combat. Only peaked caps and lace boots proved suitable; otherwise DAK soldiers made large use of captured British uniforms (especially overcoats) to which German insignia were applied.

While heat and lack of acclimatization did not cause too many problems in the beginning, troubles were encountered in 1942 as is shown by the case of the Ramcke Brigade; sent to the desert in full summer, it soon had half of its men ill. In general, however, one of the DAK soldiers' main areas of complaint was over food and water. Partly supplied by the Italians, the food did not meet the German soldiers' taste and actually became one of the main causes of illness due to a diet rich in fat and pulses and poor in vitamins. Those who did not fall ill suffered a 10 per cent weight loss that affected their physical resistance. However, these could seem like ideal conditions, since, because of supply problems, starvation was not uncommon. However, water supply was never a major problem perhaps because, as the British observed, the Germans overestimated actual consumption. As early as March–April 1941 the DAK had set up a system based on combat units carrying a four days' water supply, while many water supply units existed both to find and to transport water. These included the *schwere* and *leichte Kompanie für Wasserversorgung* (heavy water supply company, the latter with 28 vehicles), the *Kompanie für Wasserdestillation* (water distillation company, some 200 strong with 105 vehicles), the *Filterkolonne* and the *Wasserkolonne* (filter and water columns), the latter capable of carrying 60 tons of water. The use of those large and resistant canisters that, pressed into British service, became known as 'Jerrycans', also proved particularly valuable. Problems with water arose due to the fact that shortages made it very difficult for front-line soldiers to wash and because infected drinking water often provoked dysentery.

Infantry

Infantry in North Africa had the same armament as all other German infantry units. The basic weapon was the 7.92mm Karabiner 98k rifle, roughly the equivalent of the British Lee Enfield, while squad and platoon leaders were armed with the greatly admired 9mm Maschinenpistole 38 and 40 machine pistol. Heavy weapons included the 7.92mm Maschinengewehr 34 light machine gun, which, mounted on its tripod, also served as a heavy machine gun, the light 50mm Granatenwerfer 36 and the heavy 81mm Granatenwerfer 34 mortars. The well-known Stielhandgranate 24, also known as 'potato masher' or 'stick grenade', and the Eihandgranate 39, similar to the egg-shaped Mills hand grenade, were widely used. Apart from the anti-tank guns, the only weapons capable of dealing with tanks and other AFVs were the 7.92mm Panzerbüchse 38 and 39 anti-tank rifles, capable of piercing 30mm of 60-degree inclined armour at 300m. There were also anti-personnel and anti-tank mines, the latter including the renowned (and very effective) Tellermine 29 and 35 ('dish mine'), and accompanying light and heavy infantry guns; these were the 75mm leichte Infanterie Geschütz 18 and the 150mm schwere Infanterie Geschütz 33. Sand and dust caused many problems with weapons maintenance. Automatic weapons like the MP38/40 and the MG34 were the most affected, the latter in particular experiencing troubles with its cartridge belt feed. Extreme care was required and, apart from using muzzle covers, soldiers had to wrap every bolt and moving part in cloth and had to pay much attention to the use of lubricating oil (only a very thin coat of oil had to be put on moving pieces). Lack of training and practice in handling and maintaining the weapons caused certainly as many problems, if not more, than the climate.

A heavy Maschinengewehr 34 team ready to open fire from what was considered the best defensive position in the desert: a simple hole dug in the ground. The difference between light and heavy machine guns is shown by the use of the tripod, which enabled more sustained and accurate fire. (Filippo Cappellano)

In 1941 the DAK was unfortunate in having three different infantry units organizations, each one possessing a different strength and weaponry. 5.leichte Division's two *Maschinengewehre Bataillone* were particulary strong with their 46 light and heavy MGs, 9 PzB, 15 light and heavy mortars and six to 15 37mm Pak 35/36. 15.Panzer Division's Schützen Brigade had a larger amount of firepower that included (totalling both the Schützen Regiment and the Kradschützen Bataillon) 366 light and heavy MGs, 75 light and heavy mortars, 15 37mm Pak 35/36 plus six 50mm Pak 38, and 22 light and heavy IG. The divisional reorganization of September 1941 gave a better balance of firepower, with 21.Panzer Division's infantry units now fielding 132 light and 64 heavy MGs, 11 PzB, 27 light and 18 heavy mortars, nine Pak 35/36 and 19 Pak 38 plus four light and two heavy IGs. A comparison with 15.Panzer Division (it had 187 light and 78 heavy MGs, 11 PzB, 36 light and 24 heavy mortars, 12 Pak 35/36 and 10 Pak 38, six light and two heavy IGs) shows the latter was still stronger, though the difference was no longer as great. On paper at least, Afrika Division zbV's infantry firepower was superior still with 333 light and 84 heavy MGs, 148 PzB, and 42 light and 42 heavy mortars. One should keep in mind, however, that this was its only firepower since the division lacked artillery and

A line-up of mid-production PzKpfw III Ausf. Gs (Trop) belonging to the 6.Kompanie of Panzer Regiment 5 ready to parade through the streets of Tripoli. 3.Panzer Division's insignia is clearly visible on the front and left side hull armour. (Carlo Pecchi Collection)

10A: Schützen/Panzergrenadier Regiment, 1942

	Rgt-StabsKp	SchtzKp (x 4)	TOTALS – Bataillon	(13.) IG Kp	(14.) PionKp	TOTALS – Regiment
Lt MG	6	18	72	0	10	232
Hvy MG	0	2	8	0	2	26
PzB	0	3	12	0	3	39
Hvy Mtrs	0	3	12	0	3	39
Pak 38	3	3	12	0	3	42
Lt IG	0	0	0	4	0	4
Hvy IG	0	0	0	2	0	2

Figures for 90. leichte Infanterie/Afrika Division were slightly lower; each Schützen-Kompanie had an established allowance of only one Panzerbüchse and two heavy mortars. Furthermore, its regiments had no 14.(Pionier) Kompanie.

10B: A *Schützen* Regiment's total weapons strength in 1941 and 1942

	1941 Rgt	Sept 1941 Rgt	1942 Rgt
Lt MG	119	119	232
Hvy MG	28	28	26
PzB	0	2	39
Lt Mtrs	18	18	0
Hvy Mtrs	12	12	39
Pak 35/36	6	6	0
Pak 38	3	7	42
Lt IG	8	4	4
Hvy IG	2	2	2

any of the support units the two Panzer divisions had. Minor organizational changes introduced in September 1941 apart, in the same period a new weapon made its appearance: the tapered-bore heavy 28/20mm schwere Panzerbüchse 41, a light anti-tank gun capable of piercing 52mm of 30-degree inclined armour at 500m.

1942 brought many changes in infantry unit organization and firepower. Firstly, 'light' weapons – in particular mortars, light anti-tank rifles and infantry guns – were deemed unsuitable for North African warfare, either because their lightweight projectiles were not capable of piercing enemy AFV armour or because they had not much effect on the ground (sandy ground actually reduced the effect of explosive shells). Secondly, infantry units were reorganized to emphasize both their firepower and their anti-tank capabilities. *MG* and *schwere Kompanien* were disbanded and absorbed into the new *Schützen* – from late July *Panzergrenadier* – *Kompanien*, four of which now formed a battalion. The established weapon allowance of the new regiment was quite impressive considering that their allocation of light MGs was now almost twice that of the old *Schützen Regiment*, while the number of heavy MGs had only been reduced by two. Also the new regiment possessed more mortars (39 rather than 30, all heavy), and its anti-tank capabilities had been improved with its 39 PzB (mostly PzB 41) and 42 Pak 38. Already tested in January 1942 by Schützen Regiment 115, the new organization was introduced on 1 April 1942 (**Tables 10A** and **10B**). More or less at the same time, DAK units began to receive examples of the new 7.92mm Maschinengewehr 42 for evaluation, which proved to be a very effective weapon.

Panzers

The experience of the DAK proves that, in the Western Desert, the tank was the master of the battlefield. When they were sent to North Africa, both Panzer Regiment 5 and 8 were in the middle of a reorganization process that only the latter had actually completed. This included a re-equipment with the new 50mm Kwk-armed tanks and the transition to new tables of organization, issued on 1 February 1941. According to these, each *Panzer Abteilung* was composed of a *Stab*, two *leichte* and one *mittlere Panzer Kompanie*, plus a *Panzer Staffel* grouping together all available spare tanks. *Stabskompanien* included a *Nachrichtenzug* (two Panzer Befehlswagen and a PzKpfw III) and a *leichte Panzerzug* with five PzKpfw II (Panzer Regiment 5 had an extra *leichte Panzerzug* per *Abteilung* and one with the regimental HQ). *Leichte Panzerkompanien* were composed of a *Kompanietrupp* (two PzKpfw III), a *leichte Panzerzug* and three *leichte Zuge*, each with five PzKpfw III. *Mittlere Panzerkompanie* included a *Kompanietrupp* (two PzKpfw IV), a *leichte Panzerzug* and three *Zuge*, each with four PzKpfw IV. Therefore, regimental paper strength consisted of six Panzer Befehlswagen, 45 PzKpfw II (60 with Panzer Regiment 5, that had three more *leichte Panzerzuge*), 71 PzKpfw III and 28 PzKpfw IV. According to available data, when it arrived at Tripoli on 10 March 1941 Panzer Regiment 5 was almost at full strength having seven Panzer Befehlswagen, 25 PzKpfw I, 45 PzKpfw II, 61 PzKpfw III (ten others had been lost at sea) and 17 PzKpfw IV (three others lost at sea). PzKpfw I seem to have been used to make good for the lack of PzKpfw II since they actually equipped one regimental and two *Abteilung's leichte Panzerzug*, plus those in the *mittlere Panzerkompanie*. Between 8 February and 2 March 1941, Panzer Regiment 8 was re-equipped and prepared for North Africa. New PzKpfw IV and Panzer Befehlswagen were received, while 31 old PzKpfw III armed with the 37mm Kwk were replaced by the new ones armed with the 50mm Kwk (older PzKpfw II Ausf. C were also returned to the depots in exchange for the new ones). On 7 May 1941, when it arrived in North Africa, the regiment had 144 Panzers, 45 of which were light ones. Since Panzer Befehlswagen were not counted, the regiment should have been at full strength.

In 1941 the German tank inventory in North Africa included every type of tank then available, from the light PzKpfw I to the 'heavy' PzKpfw IV. With its weight of 5.4 tons and two MG34s, the PzKpfw I Ausf. A (the variant sent to North Africa) was rather more of a tankette than a tank. Built in 1934–36, it was already obsolete in 1939 and also suffered from engine breakdowns and overheating that made it extremely unreliable. Nevertheless, it saw front-line service in the Western Desert; on 30 April 1941 II./Panzer Regiment 5 (using all the running tanks left to the regiment) attacked at Ras el Mdauuar deploying 10 PzKpfw I Ausf. As, while one month later (on 25 May) the Stab II./Panzer Regiment 5 still had four PzKpfw I. On 9 October 1941, just before they disappeared (either because they became unserviceable or because they were used to provide spare parts for the Panzerjäger I), Panzer Regiment 5 still had 13 PzKpfw I. Another light tank was the PzKpfw II Ausf. C, largely used by Panzer Regiments 5 and 8. Lightweight and poorly armoured (9 tons with a

A damaged late-production PzKpfw III Ausf F armed with the 50mm Kwk 38 L/42 being loaded onto a heavy tank transport trailer towed by a heavy 18-ton tractor FAMO F2 SdKfz 9. Regimental workshops (*Panzer Werkstatt Kompanien*) did an excellent job in recovering and repairing damaged tanks. (Filippo Cappellano)

A PzKpfw IV Ausf. D of 8.Kompanie/Panzer Regiment 5 parading through the streets of Tripoli. Though it was the heaviest tank in the DAK inventory until November 1942, its 75mm Kwk 37 L/24 was of little use against enemy armour except at very short ranges. (Carlo Pecchi Collection)

maximum armour of 14.5mm), it was armed with a 20mm Kwk 30 L/55 and a single MG34. Produced until April 1940, it was obsolete as well and almost useless against enemy tanks and infantry; it was soon relegated to reconnaissance roles, though its poor speed (40kmph on a good road) made it unsuitable for this role as well.

The workhouse of the Panzer divisions in North Africa was the PzKpfw III, the principal German MBT in 1940–42. Actual delivery of the earlier models PzKpfw III Ausf. E/F to North Africa is not certain; but what is known, however, is that every PzKpfw III sent to North Africa was retrofitted and armed with the new 50mm Kwk 38 L/42 gun. The most common variant used in 1941 was the PzKpfw III Ausf. G, mounting the 50mm as a standard gun since July 1940. Its 'tropicalized' version, designated Trop (*Tropen*, tropical), mounted special ventilation and air/oil-filtering systems to protect the engine and gearbox from sand and dust. It had a limited weight (about 20 tons) and a good speed (40kmph), though it was poorly armoured with a frontal protection of only 30mm non-face hardened steel, 37mm on the gun mantlet. The PzKpfw III's 'big brother' was the PzKpfw IV, considered then a 'heavy' tank designed to provide support with its short 75mm Kwk 37 L/24. Forty PzKpfw IV Ausf. D and Es were sent to North Africa in 1941 with both Panzer Regiment 5 and 8; the latter had, in most cases, 20–30mm extra hull armour and a standard storage bin. Armour on both variants was 30mm on the front hull and up to 35mm on the gun mantlet. In spite of the adoption of Trop ventilators and filters, German tanks suffered from both the heat and sand, though the crews suffered much more than their vehicles especially during combat, when hatches had to be closed and, with an inside temperature of 45°C (113°Fahrenheit), the ventilating systems had to be shut down due to fuel shortages. On the other hand gun optical equipment proved excellent, since it functioned well even in the high temperatures and at night.

The Panzers' poor armour and their guns' poor armour-piercing capabilities caused a great deal of problems. Using the standard Panzergranate 39 (armour-piercing shell), the 50mm Kwk 38 could penetrate 54mm of homogeneous armour plate at 100m, 46mm at 500m and 36mm at 1,000m. The use of the tungsten-core PzGr 40, even more effective at close range, improved the performance as follows: 96, 58 and 42mm. The 75mm Kwk 37 was only capable of penetrating 70 to 100mm at 100m, though by using high-explosive shells (Sprenggranate) it could damage British tanks at greater distances. Early British Cruiser tanks were not much of a problem for Panzers in 1941, but the Matilda and Valentine infantry tanks, as well as the Crusader and American-produced Grant, proved formidable opponents, especially given the scarce availability of PzGr 40 and the Kwk 38's overall poor performances. Their poor armour made most of the Panzers extremely vulnerable to British anti-tank and tank guns, even at long distances (the British 2-pdr was capable of penetrating 40mm of 30-degree homogeneous armour at 800m). In December 1941 the first PzKpfw III Ausf. H arrived in North Africa, followed by the early production PzKpfw III Ausf. J and PzKpfw IV Ausf. F (the new PzKpfw II Ausf. F also arrived at the same time). Though their armament remained unchanged, their armour protection was now increased. The PzKpfw II Ausf. F's frontal armour was now 30 to 35mm, the PzKpfw III Ausf. H had a 30mm armour plate added to its 30mm standard plate while the Ausf. J had a standard 50mm frontal armour plate, like the

A heavy Flak 18 88mm getting ready to fire against a ground target while still in its towing arrangement. It equipped the Lufwaffe's *schwere Flak Batterien* (heavy anti-aircraft batteries) that, along with the *leichte Flak Batterien* armed with the 20mm Flak 38, formed a *Flak Abteilung*. Each *Abteilung* had three *schwere Batterien* for a total of 18 Flak 18 pieces. (Carlo Pecchi Collection)

PzKpfw IV Ausf. F. This increased armour neutralized the British 2-pdr gun and the adoption of wider 400mm tracks as standard (already tested with the PzKpfw III Ausf. G) made them much more mobile than ever.

From early 1942 modern Panzers began to be made available to the DAK, models really suited to tank-versus-tank combat. The first to arrive was the late-production PzKpfw III Ausf. J, similar to the earlier production models but armed with the long-barrelled 50mm Kwk 39 L/60 capable of penetrating 67 to 130mm at 100m, 57 to 72mm at 500m and 44 to 38mm at 1,000m. Used in combat for the first time at Gazala, it was available in relatively large quantities only from August 1942. It could deal on equal terms with both the Valentine and the Grant; the new long-barrelled 75mm Kwk 40 L/43 (capable of penetrating as much as 72mm

of armour plate at 1,500m) could deal on equal terms even with the American-built Sherman tank. It was used to retrofit the old PzKpfw IV Ausf. F variant that, converted as such, became known as the PzKpfw IV Ausf. F2. The first examples arrived in North Africa in June 1942, but it remained a rare beast until late summer. Both the long-barrelled PzKpfw III and IV were known as *Spezial* (special), a name the British adopted as well.

In spite of the excellent job done by tank recovery teams and by regimental *Werkstatt Kompanien*, losses due to either mechanical breakdown or combat as well as supply problems greatly reduced the number of available Panzers. As a consequence, the reorganization implemented in September 1941 saw a reduction in the established number of PzKpfw IVs, now set at ten with only two *Zuge* per each *mittlere Panzerkompanie*. Otherwise, the rest of a *Panzer Regiment*'s established strength remained unchanged (**Table 11**; **Fig. 10**). This

A *Panzerjäger Zug* during a moment of rest, in the foreground the usual Demag D7 SdKfz 10 towing a 50mm Pak 38. The fact that the vehicles only have a coat of sand over their European dark-grey colour, and also the presence of Pak 35/36 37mm guns towed by other Demags, suggests the photo was taken in early 1941 and that it probably shows elements from Panzerjäger Abteilung 39. Note the use of the *Zeltbahn* (camouflage sheet) as a sun shield. (Carlo Pecchi Collection)

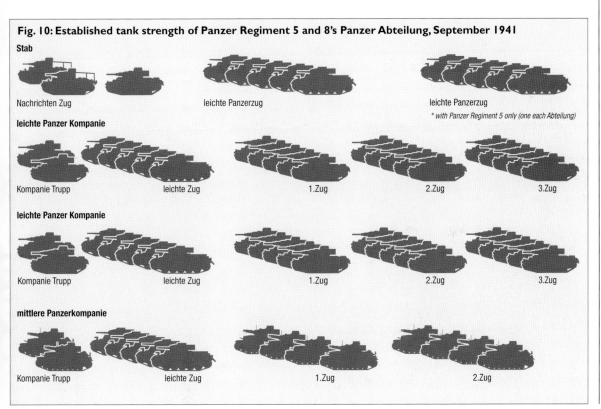

Fig. 10: Established tank strength of Panzer Regiment 5 and 8's Panzer Abteilung, September 1941

Stab

Nachrichten Zug   leichte Panzerzug   leichte Panzerzug

* with Panzer Regiment 5 only (one each Abteilung)

leichte Panzer Kompanie

Kompanie Trupp   leichte Zug   1.Zug   2.Zug   3.Zug

leichte Panzer Kompanie

Kompanie Trupp   leichte Zug   1.Zug   2.Zug   3.Zug

mittlere Panzerkompanie

Kompanie Trupp   leichte Zug   1.Zug   2.Zug

Table 11: 21.Panzer Division established strength (weapons and vehicles), September–December 1941

	Stab	Pz Rgt 5	SchtzRgt 104 St	I./SR 104	MG Batl 8	Aufkl Abt 3	ArtRgt 155	PzJäg Abt 39	PzPion Btl 200	PzNachr Abt 200	Services	TOTALS
Lt MG34	2	0	2	58	13	26	18	18	27	0	15	237
Hvy MG34	0	0	0	14	36	2	0	0	0	0	0	66
Lt Mtrs	0	0	0	9	9	3	0	0	0	0	0	30
Hvy Mtrs	0	0	0	6	6	0	0	0	0	0	0	18
Hvy PzB	0	0	0	1	9	0	0	0	0	0	0	11
Pak 35/36	0	0	0	3	6	3	0	0	0	0	0	15
Pak 38	0	0	3	2	9	3	0	18	0	0	0	37
Lt FH 18	0	0	0	0	0	0	24	0	0	0	0	24
Hvy FH 18	0	0	0	0	0	0	8	0	0	0	0	8
K 18 gun	0	0	0	0	0	0	4	0	0	0	0	4
PzKpfw II	0	59	0	0	0	0	0	0	12	0	0	71
PzKpfw III	0	111	0	0	0	0	0	0	0	0	0	111
PzKpfw IV	0	30	0	0	0	0	0	0	0	0	0	30
BefhPz 266	0	4	0	0	0	0	0	0	0	0	0	4
BefhPz 267	0	2	0	0	0	0	0	0	0	5	0	7
BefhPz 268	0	0	0	0	0	0	0	0	0	2	0	2
SdKfz 253	0	0	0	0	0	0	36	0	0	0	0	36
SdKfz 251	0	0	0	0	10	0	0	0	0	0	0	10
SdKfz 251/6	1	0	0	0	0	0	0	0	1	1	0	3
SdKfz 251/7	0	0	0	0	0	0	0	0	6	0	0	6
SdKfz 221	0	0	0	0	0	10	0	0	0	0	0	10
SdKfz 222	0	0	0	0	0	14	0	0	0	0	0	14
SdKfz 223	0	0	0	0	0	4	0	0	0	0	0	4
SdKfz 231	0	0	0	0	0	3	0	0	0	0	0	3
SdKfz 232	0	0	0	0	0	3	0	0	0	0	0	3
SdKfz 247	0	0	0	0	0	2	0	0	0	0	0	2
SdKfz 260	0	0	0	0	0	1	0	0	0	2	0	3
SdKfz 261	0	0	0	0	0	4	0	2	0	8	0	14
SdKfz 263	0	0	0	0	0	3	0	0	0	8	0	11
Motorcycle	17	172	10	69	110	130	141	48	71	16	96	949
Cars	44	82	14	43	255	75	237	54	41	24	68	980
Lorries	33	383	13	146	61	81	246	37	97	34	405	1,682
Kfz 31 Amb	0	3	1	1	2	3	0	1	1	1	38	52
Sdkfz 7	0	6	0	0	0	1	0	0	0	0	4	11
Sdkfz 9	0	8	0	0	0	0	0	0	0	0	0	8
Sdkfz 10	0	0	0	6	15	3	0	45	0	0	0	75
SdKfz 11	0	0	0	0	0	0	45	0	0	0	0	45

Notes: Totals include the entire division (that is also II./SR 104), though they still are incomplete (for example, 11.(IG)/SR 104 is not included). Figures are approximate for both weapons and non-AFVs.

Table 12: Panzer Regiment tank strength comparison, September 1941 – May 1942

Panzer Regiment established tank strength, September 1941

	Rgt Stab		I–II Panzer Abteilung		leichte Panzer Kompanie (two each Abteilung)					mittlere Panzer Kompanie				Totals – entire regiment
	Nachr Zug	le Pz Zug	Nachr Zug	le Pz Zug	Kp Tr	le Zug	1. Zug	2. Zug	3. Zug	Kp Tr	le Zug	1. Zug	2. Zug	
BefhPz	2	0	2	0	0	0	0	0	0	0	0	0	0	6
Pz II	0	5	0	5	0	5	0	0	0	0	5	0	0	45
Pz III	1	0	1	0	2	0	5	5	5	0	0	0	0	71
Pz IV	0	0	0	0	0	0	0	0	0	2	0	4	4	20

Panzer Regiment established tank strength, May 1942

	Rgt Stab		I–II Panzer Abteilung Stab			leichte Panzer Kompanie (three each Abteilung)					mittlere Panzer Kompanie					Totals – entire regiment
	Nachr Zug	le Pz Zug	Nachr Zug	Pz le Zug	Pi Zug	Kp Tr	1. Zug	2. Zug	3. Zug	4. Zug	Kp Tr	le Zug	1. Zug	2. Zug	3. Zug	
BefhPz	2	0	2	0	0	0	0	0	0	0	0	0	0	0	0	6
Pz II	0	5	0	5	2	0	0	0	0	0	0	5	0	0	0	29
Pz III	1	0	1	0	0	2	5	5	5	5	0	0	0	0	0	135
Pz IV	0	0	0	0	0	0	0	0	0	0	2	0	3	3	3	22

Note: There were minor differences between Panzer Regiment 5 and 8 since the former had three more leichte Panzerzug, one with the Regiments Stab and one attached to the Stab of each Abteilung (whose Stabskompanie already included one leichte Panzerzug), for a total of 15 more PzKpfw II.

organization and weapons' allocation had proven unsuitable for the large armour-versus-armour battles that characterized the war in the Western Desert and was therefore changed again. The established tank strength introduced in April 1942 for both Panzer Regiment 5 and 8, which saw minor changes until mid-May, marked a definitive increase in both the availability and quality of Panzers (**Table 12, Fig. 11**). *Leichte Kompanie's leichte Zuge* were transformed into ordinary *Panzer Zuge* and equipped with PzKpfw III, thus increasing the total number of medium tanks in a regiment from 71 to 135. This increase had also been made possible by the decision to bring to three the number of *leichte Kompanien* in a *Panzer Abteilung*, which was effectively carried out in early 1942. In the meantime the number of PzKpfw II fell down from 45 to 29, two of which were used to equip the *Panzer Abteilung's Pionier Zug*. Only the number of PzKpfw IV remained below authorized strengths, since DAK's Panzer Divisions only had 11 per *mittlere Kompanie* rather than 14. The overall marked increase in tank strengths, as well as the new models available, played a major role in DAK's victories in spring and summer 1942.

Anti-tank and anti-aircraft weapons

Discussion of German anti-tank and anti-aircraft weapons in North Africa often centres around the dreaded 88mm Flak gun that, in spite of its fame, was actually not that widely used. No more than 30–40 could ever be deployed at

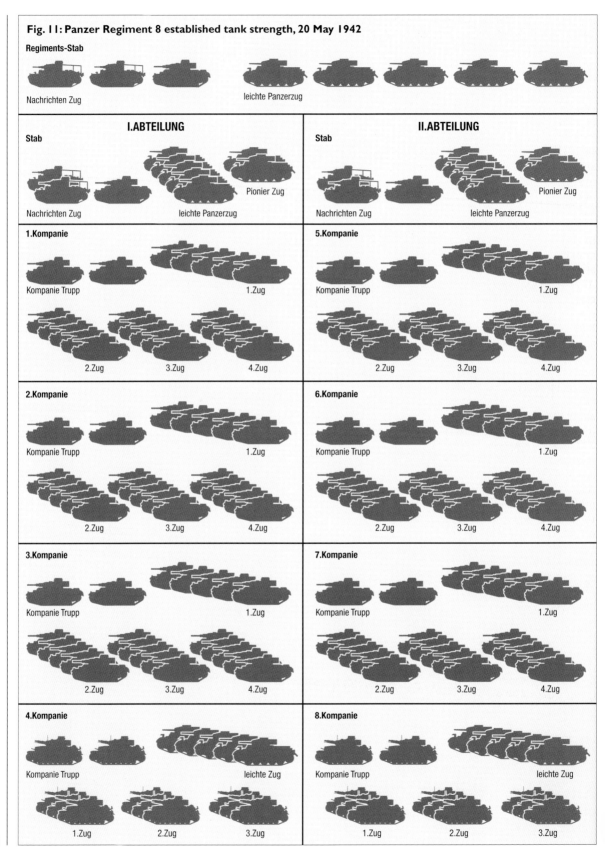

Fig. 11: Panzer Regiment 8 established tank strength, 20 May 1942

Regiments-Stab

Nachrichten Zug

leichte Panzerzug

I.ABTEILUNG

Stab

Nachrichten Zug

leichte Panzerzug

Pionier Zug

II.ABTEILUNG

Stab

Nachrichten Zug

leichte Panzerzug

Pionier Zug

1.Kompanie

Kompanie Trupp

1.Zug

2.Zug

3.Zug

4.Zug

5.Kompanie

Kompanie Trupp

1.Zug

2.Zug

3.Zug

4.Zug

2.Kompanie

Kompanie Trupp

1.Zug

2.Zug

3.Zug

4.Zug

6.Kompanie

Kompanie Trupp

1.Zug

2.Zug

3.Zug

4.Zug

3.Kompanie

Kompanie Trupp

1.Zug

2.Zug

3.Zug

4.Zug

7.Kompanie

Kompanie Trupp

1.Zug

2.Zug

3.Zug

4.Zug

4.Kompanie

Kompanie Trupp

leichte Zug

1.Zug

2.Zug

3.Zug

8.Kompanie

Kompanie Trupp

leichte Zug

1.Zug

2.Zug

3.Zug

the same time: Flak Regiment 135 had 36 of them in May and 39 in August 1942. Much of its fame actually derives from the lack of suitable purpose-built anti-tank weapons in 1941. Before 5.leichte Division left for Tripoli the OKH ordered its Panzerjäger Abteilung 39 to exchange its new 50mm Pak 38 for the old 37mm Pak 35/36, though it was eventually left with a single Pak 38-armed *Zug* per *Kompanie*. In early 1941 both Panzer divisions only had a limited anti-tank capability partly mitigated by the presence of Panzerjäger Abteilung 605 (sfl)'s self-propelled anti-tank guns. However, soon both Panzerjäger Abteilung 33 and 39 began to exchange their old Pak 35/36, with the new Pak 38, with the former handed over to the units forming Afrika Division zbV. Between May and September 1941 the number of Pak 38s in each *Panzerjäger Abteilung* increased from nine to 12, and, by 20 September, both had handed over all of their Pak 35/36s, though Panzerjäger Abteilung 33 was still not up to full strength (**Fig. 12**).

Although still prevalent in 1941/42, the 37mm Pak 35/36 was outdated even in 1939. Though an excellent gun in the mid-1930s, in the early 1940s its armour-piercing capabilities – 29mm of 30-degree homogeneous armour plate at 500m – rendered it virtually useless, unless used against lightly armoured AFVs. The introduction of the PzGr 40 and eventually the development, in early 1942, of the muzzle-loaded Stielgranate 41 brought no real improvement since the Pak 35/36's effectiveness was still limited to 100m. On the other hand, the 50mm Pak 38 was a superb weapon, though not very effective against heavy armour. Weighing less than a ton and just 1.1m metres high it was a sturdy, reliable and easy to handle weapon. Not easy to detect, it was superior to the British 2-pdr because of its greater armour-piercing capabilities. At 100m it could penetrate 69mm of 30-degree homogeneous armour plate (130mm using the PzGr 40), which became 59/72mm at 500m and 48/38mm at 1,000m. Able to deal with most of the British armour in the Western Desert, it remained the German standard anti-tank gun until late 1942 along with the 76.2mm Pak 36(r), mainly used by 90.leichte Division's units.

In the early war years not much attention had been paid to self-propelled anti-tank guns. The development of the 47mm Pak (t) L/43 (sfl) auf PzKpfw I Ausf. B appears to have been a belated attempt to make better use of the otherwise obsolete PzKpfw I chassis. With only 202 produced from March 1940 to February 1941, it was armed with a Czech-produced anti-tank gun capable of penetrating 54mm of 30-degree armour plate at 100m (100mm with the PzGr 40), which became 48/59mm at 500m and 41mm at 1,000m (PzGr 40 was

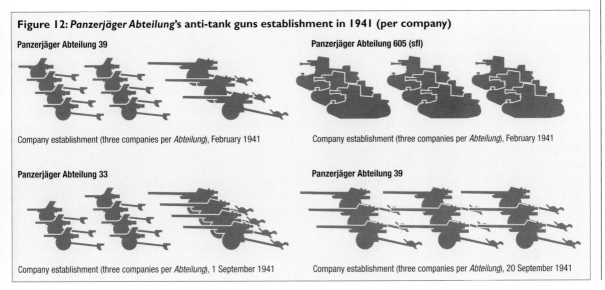

Figure 12: *Panzerjäger Abteilung's* anti-tank guns establishment in 1941 (per company)

Panzerjäger Abteilung 39

Company establishment (three companies per *Abteilung*), February 1941

Panzerjäger Abteilung 605 (sfl)

Company establishment (three companies per *Abteilung*), February 1941

Panzerjäger Abteilung 33

Company establishment (three companies per *Abteilung*), 1 September 1941

Panzerjäger Abteilung 39

Company establishment (three companies per *Abteilung*), 20 September 1941

In a featureless terrain like the Western Desert, even standing on top of a tank was helpful for observation. A 47mm Pak (t) L/43 (sfl) auf PzKpfw I Ausf. B (or simply Panzerjäger I) in the desert. These equipped Panzerjäger Abteilung 605 (sfl), and were still in use in October 1942. (Carlo Pecchi Collection)

no longer effective at this range). Used to equip Panzerjäger Abteilung 605 (sfl), whose 1941 establishment was of 27 vehicles, it was not the best solution but the only one available. Battlefield experience soon suggested a number of improvements. An ingenious and impromptu solution was found by combining together the chassis of an obsolete tank and a powerful anti-tank gun, in this case the Soviet 76.2mm gun, which the Germans had captured en masse (along with ammunition) during the first months of their advance into the Soviet Union, Mounted on the chassis of the PzKpfw 38(t) it created the Panzerjäger 38(t) für 7,62 cm Pak 36(r) (SdKfz 139), also known as Marder III, the first of a long and successful series of self-propelled anti-tank guns.

Produced between April and October 1942, the Panzerjäger 38(t) was perhaps the most powerful anti-tank weapon ever used by the DAK. Although the vehicle was rather heavy and high (about 11 tons and 2.5m high), it was well armoured (50mm on hull and superstructure) and was armed with a very powerful weapon capable of penetrating 98mm of 30-degree homogeneous armour plate at 100m (135mm using the PzGr 40), 90 and 116mm at 500m, 82 and 94mm at 1,000m. 73 and 75mm at 1,500m and 65 and 58mm at 2,000m – enough to make it a real 'tankbuster' in the desert.

Availability was, however, the real problem since only 66 were sent to North Africa between July 1942 and May 1943. Initially used to equip both Panzerjäger Abteilung 33 and 39, the first examples only arrived in late summer and went to the first companies of both *Abteilungen*, which became the self-propelled anti-tank companies. There were not enough Panzerjäger 38(t) to equip both companies, and the second one remained equipped with the towed Pak 38 (**Fig. 13**). Scarce availability of this weapon was certainly one of the reasons that prevented Panzerjäger Abteilung 605 (sfl) from being equipped with them until at least mid-October 1942. The gap was filled thanks to the development of an even more ad-hoc solution. In mid-October 1941 the OKH ordered the fast development of a more powerful self-propelled anti-tank gun for the DAK using the Soviet 76.2mm Pak 36(r). A suitable solution was found by mounting the gun on a Büssing-NAG BN9 5-ton halftracked vehicle, producing the 76.2mm FK 36(r) auf Panzerjäger Selbsfahrlafette Zugkraftwagen 5t, otherwise known as 'Diana'. A rather clumsy vehicle about 3m high, the first six examples were sent

A *Zug* of Panzerjäger 38(t) für 7,62 cm PAK 36(r) (SdKfz 139) (Marder III) resting under the palms of a desert oasis. Although just a makeshift solution, this self-propelled anti-tank gun proved extremely reliable and effective, eventually giving birth to a whole series of self-propelled Panzerjäger. (Carlo Pecchi Collection)

Fig. 13: Actual strength of Panzerjäger Abteilung 33, 23 October 1942

2.Kompanie

1.Kompanie

to North Africa in January 1942, followed by three others in February (only nine were produced in total). All were used to equip Panzerjäger Abteilung 605 (sfl), which formed mixed *Panzerjäger Kompanien* using the Diana and the Panzerjäger I (**Fig. 14**). Seven examples of the Diana were used at Gazala with good results (on 28 May one of them stopped the 4th Armoured Brigade at El Adem), but their number was soon reduced. By mid-June 1942, before Panzerjäger Abteilung 605 (sfl) was withdrawn to Bardia for rest and refitting, only two Dianas were left, though apparently three were still available in August. To fully understand how important these lesser-known weapons were in comparison with the famous 88mm it is worth considering that on 21 October 1942 15.Panzer Division only had eight 88mm Flak guns, but 72 50mm Pak 38 and 16 76.2mm self-propelled Panzerjäger 38(t).

A leichte Panzerspähwagen (2cm) SdKfz 222 in an apparently staged photo to show its 20mm Kwk 30/38 used in an anti-aircraft role. Poorly armoured and excessively lightweight, the SdKfz 222 did not prove a suitable vehicle for desert warfare. (Carlo Pecchi Collection)

The Flak 30 and 38 20mm anti-aircraft gun mounted on the 1-ton half-tracked Demag D7 tractor (designated 2cm Flak auf Fahrgestell Zugkraftwagen 1t (SdKfz 10/4)) was perhaps the most common and effective anti-aircraft weapon used by the DAK, although the 88mm Flak 36/37 and 41 were also used in the same role. Amongst others, the former equipped Fla Bataillon 606 (sfl) in rather large quantities, and was also widely used by the Befehls Staffel. The only three examples of the Sturmgeschütz III destined to serve in North Africa before November 1942 certainly deserve a last word. These three Ausf. Ds were part of Sonderverband 288, whose inventory shows all of them were available on 25 May 1942. However, they did not last long: either because of enemy action or mechanical breakdown, they were lost during the Gazala battles and by 1 July none were available.

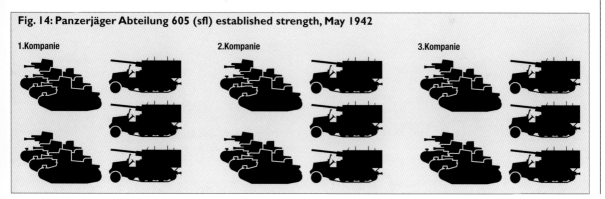

Fig. 14: Panzerjäger Abteilung 605 (sfl) established strength, May 1942

1.Kompanie

2.Kompanie

3.Kompanie

An SdKfz 250/1 armed with a French 25mm Hotchkiss light anti-tank gun. In early May 1942 Panzer Aufklärungs Abteilung 33 received ten of these, which were used to form two *Zuge* (each one with five vehicles) in its *schwere Kompanie*. (Carlo Pecchi Collection)

A *leichte Batterie* equipped with 105mm leichte Feldhaubitze 18 howitzers is ready to open fire (note the 3-ton Hanomag 11 kl 6 SdKfz 11 half-tracks in the background). This howitzer was inferior to its British equivalent, the 25-pdr. (Carlo Pecchi Collection)

Vehicles and other AFVs

For a motorized corps like the DAK, the availability and efficiency of motor vehicles was a crucial factor. Established allotment of motor vehicles for a late 1941 Panzer division numbered about 3,500–4,000 (**Table 11**). Most of them, about 90 per cent of the total, were non-combat wheeled vehicles used to transport men and supplies. 21.Panzer Division's vehicle establishment in late December 1941 included almost 1,000 motorcycles (of which more than 700 were combination), still largely used by combat units in spite of their unsuitability for desert warfare. On the other hand the division had about 1,000 cars, a figure including about 450 small staff cars like the Kübelwagen (Kfz 1 to 4 models), about 350 medium staff cars (Kfz 12, 17), about 15 heavy staff cars (Kfz 21 and 23) and more than 150 off-road light trucks for personnel transport like the Krupp Protze (Kfz 69, 70 and 81), as well as 52 Kfz 31 ambulances. The greatest part of the *c*.1,700 lorries, mainly used by the artillery and service and supply units, was made up of medium lorries, only some of which were four-wheel drives like the Opel 'Blitz'. Being an armoured division it also had a large allocation of half-tracked vehicles, only some of which were attached to combat units. As a matter of fact only a small fraction of DAK's infantry was mounted in armoured personnel carriers (*gepanzert Mannschafts Transport Wagen*, MTW). In February 1941 the *Stabskompanien* of both *MG Bataillone* was allotted ten SdKfz 251/1 ('Hanomag') MTW, while only 2./Schützen Regiment 115 of the 15.Panzer Division was mounted in MTWs as well. In December 1941, 21.Panzer Division only had ten armoured SdKfz 251 troop carriers, while all other half-tracked vehicles were used in other roles. The SdKfz 251/6 was a command vehicle, 251/7 a *Pionier* vehicle and the SdKfz 253 a light armoured observation vehicle. Most halftracks were simply tractors mainly used by Artillerie Regiment 155 and Panzerjäger Abteilung 39 to transport their guns (the SdKfz 7 was an 8-ton tractor, the SdKfz 9 18 tons, the SdKfz 10 a light 1-ton tractor and the SdKfz 11 a 3-ton tractor). There was actually a larger allocation of wheeled combat vehicles than wheeled armoured vehicles, including 64 armoured cars (*Panzerspähwagen*) mainly used by the Aufklärungs Abteilung 3. These included the four-wheeled SdKfz 221 (light AC armed with MGs), SdKfz 222 (a 20mm gun-armed AC) and SdKfz 223 (light command AC), the six wheeled SdKfz 247 (command AC) and SdKfz 261 (radio command AC), as well as the eight-wheeled SdKfz 231 (20mm gun-armed AC), SdKfz 232 (radio command AC) and SdKfz 263 (radio command AC). There were also 13 Befehls Panzer (derived from the PzKpfw III) SdKfz 266, 267 and 268, used by both Panzer Regiment 5 and Panzer Nachrichten Abteilung 200 (**Table 13**).

Vehicles were always a problem for the DAK, first because of their shortage and also because of the many problems they faced in the desert. The OKH was behind one of these problems since, without caring to check whether the Italians used diesel-fuelled vehicles or not (they actually did with great success), it decided to avoid problems caused by having vehicles using two different types of fuel and initially only sent petrol-fuelled vehicles to North Africa, thus limiting their number and quality. The result was that many two-wheel drive vehicles were used by the DAK, either derived from civilian models or even civilian models pressed into military service, and they were particularly unsuited to the desert. To have an idea of the proportion, in summer 1941 out of 1,000 lorries used by the 15.Panzer Division

Table 13: Panzerarmee Afrika AFVs established strength, November 1942

	Pz AOK	Arko 104	DAK	15.PzDiv	21.PzDiv	90.lei.	(present) TOTALS
SdKfz 221	0	0	0	10	10	0	20 (4)
SdKfz 222	0	0	0	7	14	0	21 (12)
SdKfz 223	0	0	0	4	4	0	8 (4)
SdKfz 231	0	0	0	3	3	0	6 (2)
SdKfz 232	0	0	0	3	3	0	6 (2)
SdKfz 247	0	0	0	2	2	0	4 (0)
SdKfz 250	0	0	0	2	2	0	4 (1)
SdKfz 250/3	0	0	0	2	2	0	4 (1)
SdKfz 251	0	0	0	33	31	0	64 (15)
SdKfz 251/6	1	0	0	4	3	1	9 (0)
SdKfz 254	0	0	0	22	7	0	29 (2)
SdKfz 260	0	0	0	3	4	0	7 (2)
SdKfz 261	0	11	0	29	29	0	69 (12)
SdKfz 263	1	0	0	16	16	0	33 (2)

only 45 were four-wheel drive. In the same period, 21.Panzer Division's *Nachschubkolonne* only had 74 lorries suitable for desert terrain. The strain imposed by the lack of paved roads and by sand, dust and heat had impressive effects on German vehicles that, as opposed to British ones, had not been designed for tropical use. The sturdy Kübelwagen was much loved and proved an extremely useful and reliable vehicle, especially when equipped with the large, over-sized aircraft tyres, yet – in spite of the special filters adopted – its engine only had a lifetime of 12,000–14,000km (5,000km before the adoption of special filters), that is about one-fifth of its normal lifetime (60,000–70,000km). In comparison, a tank needed a new engine every 3,500km, which was about half of its normal lifetime (7,000–8,000km). Springs also suffered heavily, in particular those of the Kfz 17, which proved extremely prone to breaking. As a consequence many vehicles were soon out of service, thus limiting actual availability: in August 1941 21.Panzer Division's supply columns only had 191 serviceable lorries out of an established strength of 315; the other 124 were under repair. In January 1942 the division lacked 2,459 vehicles (625 motorcycles, 565 cars, 831 lorries, 151 tractors and 287 AFVs) out of an established strength of 3,528; over 70 per cent were unserviceable.

Lack of half-tracked armoured vehicles was also a major problem, especially in 1942. Even the few issued to infantry units were withdrawn and used as command and communication vehicles, leaving only a few SdKfz 250s in use by the newly formed *Aufklärungs Abteilung's leichte Schützen Späh Kompanie* (in early May 1942 Aufklärungs Abteilung 33 was to receive 25 of them). Some of them were also modified by having a French-built 25mm Hotchkiss anti-tank gun mounted to improve the anti-tank capabilities of those units. Generally speaking it is no exaggeration to say that the DAK relied heavily on the use of captured British vehicles, always used in large quantities. In the summer of 1942 about half of the DAK's vehicle inventory was made up of captured vehicles, and without them Rommel would have had great difficulty in carrying his offensive into Egypt.

A 150mm schwere Feldhaubitze 18 towed by an 8-ton Krauss-Maffei KM m II SdKfz 7 tractor. The DAK always suffered from its lack of artillery, and the large use of French guns (partly acquired in Tunisia from the Vichy government) was an attempt to make good this lack. (Carlo Pecchi Collection)

Command, control, communications and intelligence (C3I)

An efficient C3I complex is of foremost importance in mobile warfare, especially in difficult terrain like the Western Desert. To master the battlefield both sides needed a practical command system, an adequate control of their own units, a workable communications net and a good view of the other side of the hill, which implies an efficient intelligence service. Most of the German C3I systems in North Africa were similar to those used in Europe, yet some particular aspects need to be highlighted.

Command

The German approach to command was based on what is (incorrectly) called *Auftragstaktik*, 'mission tactics'. It was actually a system based on the 'mission command' principle that saw senior commanders giving their subordinates only an objective to attain. They then left them the choice of how to attain it, which they had to do using their own initiative and knowledge of both the terrain and of their own unit. Such a system was in open contrast to the one called 'top-down command', ruled by rigid and detailed orders specifying both the objective and the way to attain it – a method widely used by British forces in North Africa. Though apparently superior, the 'mission command' principle was a two-edged sword since it required good, if not excellent, field commanders and a workable control system. Without an adequate control system, flexibility, which is one of the main advantages of the 'mission command system', could easily turn the battlefield into chaos. This is the reason staff work is so important, and it is no exaggeration to say that the German staff in North Africa were excellent.

Rommel had his own particular approach to the 'mission command' principle, one that actually enhanced another principle emphasized by German doctrine: commanders were to lead from the front. This was the only way a commander could properly evaluate the situation on the battlefield and acquire a good knowledge of both the terrain and his enemy, which enabled him to react swiftly to any unexpected event. A commander facing a superior enemy could choose a different approach into battle, while a commander facing a weak enemy could take full advantage of success obtained on the

Although this photo was probably taken in spring 1941 (note the captured Dorchester ACV, apparently the one used by Rommel and renamed 'Moritz'), this is what a Panzer *Befehls Staffel* on the march must have looked like. In the foreground is an SdKfz 10/4 self-propelled 20mm anti-aircraft gun. (Filippo Cappellano)

battlefield. In a word: flexibility, which is the capability to properly assess the situation and to arrange the most suitable solution to attain the objective. German commanders excelled in this and many of their successes (mainly in 1942) can be ascribed to their capabilities. An interesting feature specifically aimed at helping them to lead their units from the front was the development of the *Befehls Staffel* (command detachment), clearly a consequence of the experiences in North Africa during Operation *Crusader*, when DAK's HQ was overrun by British troops. The use of an advanced and a rear command echelon was a common practice with German HQs. The commander, along with the operations and intelligence officers, spearheaded his units while administrative and supply-concerned parts of the staff moved in the rear. The innovation introduced by Rommel was the creation of a small, highly mobile and well-armed support unit specifically designated to escort the advanced echelon with the purpose of protecting it against enemy actions, including air attack (**Table 14**).

German and Italian officers walking to a high-level conference. From left to right: Generalmajor Alfred Gause, Panzerarmee Afrika's chief-of-staff, Generaloberst Erwin Rommel, General Ugo Cavallero, Italian chief-of-general-staff, and General Curio Barbasetti, Italian liaison officer. (Archivio Ufficio Storico Stato Maggiore Esercito)

In spite of this improvement, only introduced in April 1942, DAK's officers paid a heavy price for their 'lead from the front' principle and the high level of losses suffered by German officers was not always easy to replace. Between 18 November 1941 and 20 February 1942 21.Panzer Division had 47 officers killed, 61 wounded and 40 missing; it is worth noting officers represented 10 per cent of all killed, but only 4 per cent of all wounded and 2 per cent of all missing. Figures for the period 21 May–20 September 1942 are similar, with 57 officers killed (7.5 per cent of all killed), 214 wounded (7.4 per cent, but 59 of them lightly) and 17 missing (2.4 per cent). The pattern, showing how officers were more likely to be killed than wounded or captured, was repeated across the other divisions. Losses suffered by 90.leichte Afrika Division between November 1941 and 31 March 1942 included 27 officers dead (7.6 per cent of the total), 27 wounded (3.6 per cent) and 86 missing (2.3 per cent). Between 20 October and 21 November 1942 15.Panzer Division had 13 officers killed (7 per cent), 28 wounded (5.8 per cent) and 29 missing (3 per cent).

Most noticeably, those figures also included high-ranking officers. Generalleutnant Ludwig Crüwell, who succeeded Rommel as DAK's CO on 15 August 1941, was shot down and captured during a reconnaissance flight on 29 May 1942. His successor, General der Panzertruppe Walther K. Nehring, was wounded at Tobruk on 31 August 1942. DAK's command was then held for a brief period by Generalmajor von Vaerst (see below) and then, from 17 September 1942, by General der Panzertruppe Wilhelm von Thoma, who was captured at El Alamein on 4 November. Casualties were even higher with divisional commanders: Generalmajor Johann von Ravenstein, the successor of

Table 14: *Befehls Staffel*										
	SdKfz 222	SdKfz 10	SdKfz 10/4	Pak 38	Offs	NCOs	ORs	Rifles	MPs	LMGs
Gruppe Führer	0	0	0	0	1	1	3	3	1	0
Pz-Späh Zug	3	0	0	0	1	2	8	2	0	0
PzJäg Zug	0	5	0	3	1	5	32	19	4	3
Fla Zug	0	0	4	0	1	6	40	27	0	1
Gefechtstross	0	0	0	0	0	2	5	6	0	0
Totals	3	5	4	3	4	16	88	57	5	4

Soldiers busy with paperwork at a command position built beside an eight-wheeled Panzerfunkwagen SdKfz 263. A sturdy and reliable vehicle, it was used to equip divisional *Nachrichten Abteilungen*. Its only shortcoming was its scarcity, since demand always outstripped supply. (Carlo Pecchi Collection)

Generalmajor Johannes Streich, 5.leichte Division's first commander (relieved by Rommel on 22 July 1941), was captured on 29 November 1941. The most famous commander of 21.Panzer Division, Generalmajor Georg von Bismarck (who succeeded Generalleutnant Karl Böttcher), was first wounded on 17 July 1942 and, back with the division some days later, he was eventually killed in action on 31 August 1942, and Generalmajor Heinz von Randow, who became CO on 18 September, was killed on 21 December 1942. The record of 15.Panzer Division is not much different: its first CO, Generalmajor Heinrich von Prittwitz und Gaffron, was killed on 10 April 1941 and his successor, Oberst (then Generalmajor) Hans-Karl von Esebeck, was wounded on 25 July 1941. Generalmajor Walter Neumann-Silkow, who took over from him, was wounded himself on 6 December 1941, as was Generalleutnant Gustav von Vaerst on 26 May 1942 at Gazala. Generalmajor Heinz von Randow, CO from 8 July, had better luck since he was transferred on 17 September 1942, like Generalleutnant Gustav von Vaerst who, back with the division, went on sick leave on 11 November. 90.leichte Afrika Division's first commander, Generalmajor Max Sümmermann, was killed on 10 December 1941, while Generalmajor Ulrich Kleeman, CO from 21 June 1942, was wounded on 8 September 1942.

Casualty rates amongst lower units were similar. Between November 1941 and September 1942 90.leichte Division's Panzergrenadier Regiment 361 had three different commanders; one of them was killed and another one severely wounded. In the same period II./PzGrenRgt 361 had four commanders; one of them was wounded while two others were replaced because of sickness. The worst record belongs to 7.Kompanie: three out of nine of its commanders (temporary ones included) were killed, while two others were missing in action.

A Panzerbefehlswagen III Ausf. H SdKfz 267 of 15.Panzer Division (note divisional insignia to the left of DAK's insignia on the front hull plate) belonging to the Stab of Panzer Regiment 8 (note the large 'R' on the turret). The fact that it is sporting a divisional pennant on its radio antenna suggests it might have been used as a divisional command vehicle. Apparently this is an SdKfz 267 version, equipped with both FuG 6 and 8. (Carlo Pecchi Collection)

Control

Staff officers' work was certainly safer than that of their commanders, though no less important. Apart from maintaining their units in working order, they had to assure that commanders maintained control of their units and therefore mastery of the battlefields. This required handling a continuous stream of reports from both the subordinate units and their own intelligence, whose evaluation was designed to produce a (more or less accurate) overall view of the actual situation on the battlefield. Their commanders used it to prepare their own plans, and eventually to issue their orders. A peculiar problem encountered in North Africa was the difficulty in assuring tight control of large units operating in a featureless terrain like the Western Desert. Formations often broke down or took a different route and, especially in 1941, untrained officers proved unable to accurately establish their own position. As a consequence staff officers could not produce an accurate view of the situation, and commanders had problems in issuing their orders. Improved training was one solution and the use of small, purpose-built units was another.

Actually the German Army made extensive use of the *Kampfgruppe* (battlegroup), ad hoc formations that offered many advantages, amongst them ease of control. North Africa was no exception, and *Kampfgruppen* were widely used on many occasions. A closer look at their different typologies reveals how they too were ruled by the principle of flexibility. The simplest *Kampfgruppe* was the one built out of a single unit, either supported by other minor units or not. In May–June 1942, during the Gazala battles, 90.leichte Division formed several *Kampfgruppen* simply by having its battalions redesignated after their commanders' name (e.g., Pionier Bataillon 900 was known as Kampfgruppe Kube after its commander, Hauptmann Kube). In some other cases, single battalions or regiments would form a *Kampfgruppe* along with minor support units; on 5 January 1942 Kampfgruppe Ballerstedt (named after Oberstleutnant Ballerstedt) was formed using Kradschützen Bataillon 15 and a series of support units including a company from Panzerjäger Abteilung 33, a platoon from I./Flak Abteilung 33, a company from Panzer Pionier Bataillon 33, a battery from II./Artillerie Regiment 33 and a signal detachment.

Other *Kampfgruppen* were more complex since they were formed from a variety of units, often for specific combat purposes. In late March 1942, 15.Panzer Division created two different *Kampfgruppen* to man a portion of the German defensive line facing El Agheila; these included the Aufklärungsverband (reconnaissance formation) Eleba and Kampfgruppe Geissler. Both encompassed a mixture of HQ, infantry, anti-tank/armoured, artillery and communications units. (Aufklärungsverband Eleba had Stab II./SR 115, the reinforced 6./SR 115, 2./Artillerie Regiment 33 and 3.Panzerjäger Abteilung 33. Kampfgruppe Geissler had Stab Schützen Regiment 115, I./SR 115, I./Panzer Regiment 8, 1./Artillerie Regiment 33 and 1./Panzerjäger Abteilung 33.) Although the use of such mixed *Kampfgruppen* created balanced units capable of reproducing a kind of miniature Panzer division, it is interesting to note that this was not the most preferred solution. Rather, the choice fell in most cases upon a *Kampfgruppe* composed of a single, reinforced sub-unit, which, if required, could always cooperate with other *Kampfgruppen* from the same division. The example in **Fig. 15** clearly shows how that system worked within a single division when it was broken down into multiple *Kampfgruppen*, each one just little more than a single sub-unit. On 21 November 1941, during Operation *Crusader*, 15.Panzer Division broke down into three *Kampfgruppen* before moving to Bir Chatria following three different paths. Each *Kampfgruppe* had a peculiar composition and a determined role though, when needed, they could cooperate supporting each other. Kampfgruppe A, built around Panzer Regiment 8 and reinforced by two *Artillerie Abteilung*, was led by the divisional HQs and had its own communications. While this acted as a spearhead, Kampfgruppe B, built around Schützen Regiment 115 (adequately reinforced by Panzer Pionier Bataillon 33 and with the support of Panzerjäger Abteilung 33's anti-tank guns and of II./Artillerie Regiment 33's artillery), was the main support unit, though it could also fight alone as well. Kampfgruppe C, built around Regiments Stab 200 zbV, was a predominantly infantry unit that could either support the others or seize and secure any area they had captured. Both Kampfgruppe A and B began to move to Bir Chatria at 1200hrs on 21 November, while Kampfgruppe C followed one hour later (the rest of the division moved

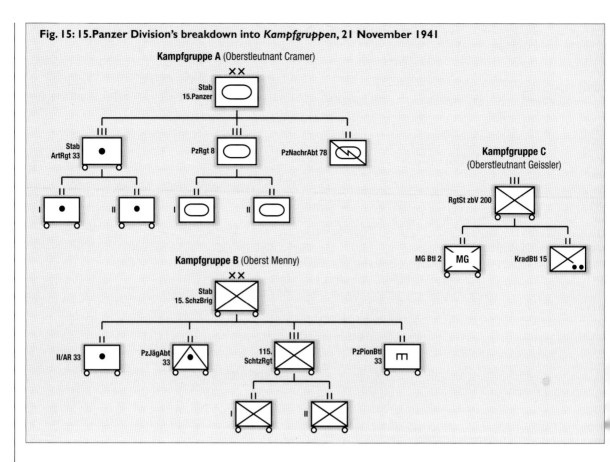

Fig. 15: 15.Panzer Division's breakdown into *Kampfgruppen*, 21 November 1941

Kampfgruppe A (Oberstleutnant Cramer)

Stab 15.Panzer

Stab ArtRgt 33 | PzRgt 8 | PzNachrAbt 78

I | II | I | II

Kampfgruppe C (Oberstleutnant Geissler)

RgtSt zbV 200

MG Btl 2 — MG | KradBtl 15

Kampfgruppe B (Oberst Menny)

Stab 15. SchzBrig

II/AR 33 | PzJägAbt 33 | 115. SchtzRgt | PzPionBtl 33

I | II

at 0300hrs on 22 November). In spite of this hurried arrangement, the night marching, poor road conditions and enemy activity, by 0730hrs on 22 November all three *Kampfgruppen* had reached their targets without problems.

Communications

In fast, mobile warfare communications were essential for both command and control. In 1941–42 the German field communications systems and equipment were the most advanced in Europe, though in North Africa some shortcomings were experienced. The use of radio communications apt for mobile units moving in the desert was not without its problems. In some cases, as during Rommel's 'dash to the wire' in November 1941, the short range of radio equipment caused contact to be lost. Also, to make radios mobile appropriate communications vehicles were needed, which the DAK were always short of. Moreover, radio communications could be intercepted by enemy's signal intelligence, and often they could be deciphered as well. On the other hand, field telephones and wire communications were more functional and reliable, though lacking the flexibility of the radio communication. That was especially true in the Western Desert, where large spaces and the limited availability of a local wire communications net strongly limited their use. For example, that only from early 1942 did Panzergruppe Afrika's communications largely rely on wire communications. Just before the attack against the Gazala Line Panzergruppe Afrika's communications net largely based on wire, and it was also ready to be moved forward as soon as the advance began. In practice, Panzerarmee's HQ served as a kind of giant switchboard connecting all the subordinate units and commands through its communications systems. In particular, those at the front line were connected using both the wire and the radio communications nets since they would have clearly lost most of their wire links after the advance. Worth noting, both Rommel's Befehls Staffel and the Panzerarmee's Kampfstaffel only used the radio communications net. Though functional in most cases, the system had some serious shortcomings. For example, only the Panzerarmee and DAK's HQs, plus ArKo 104, had a direct link with the Fliegerverbindungs Offizier, the Luftwaffe's liaison officer. Yet, German troops in North Africa were well aware of how important a direct link with Luftwaffe units was, especially to contact the close-support Stuka aircraft and the aerial reconnaissance. A system of visual signals was used, though without great success. Only in March 1942 did Rommel order the creation of a number of *Flieger Funk Truppe*, land-to-air

An Auto Union/Horch Kfz 17 communications car belonging to the Nachrichten Zug of Panzer Aufklärungs Abteilung 3 (see tactical sign on the left mudguard) parades through the streets of Tripoli. This vehicle was used by *Nachrichten Zuge* in a wide variety of different arrangements, either for radio or wire communications. (Carlo Pecchi Collection)

radio communications squads destined to serve with several divisional and regimental HQs. However, the lack of suitable vehicles, one of the DAK's greatest shortcomings, prevented their widespread use.

Wheeled communications vehicles were not much suited for front-line service, especially when moving off-road and under enemy artillery fire. In particular, the special-purpose radio vehicle Kfz 17 was especially prone to breaking springs. Half and fully tracked vehicles were preferred, though they were always in short supply and in early 1942 the *Schützen Kompanien* were stripped of them to equip the divisional *Nachrichten Abteilungen*. Mostly equipped with the Funkgerät 7, a 20-watt radio with a range of 50km, the various SdKfz 250 and 251 variants worked along with the Panzerbefehlswagen III SdKfz 267 and 268 equipped with the Funkgerät 8, a 30-watt radio with a similar range. Limited range was one serious shortcoming. The arrangement of the communication net was another one. The example in **Diagram 1** reveals that only divisional HQs could directly contact subordinate units, while neighbouring units, like those giving and receiving fire support, had to contact each other through higher HQs. For example, if either Kradschützen Bataillon 15 or MG Bataillon 2 wanted direct fire support from Artillerie Regiment 33, their request had to pass through both the Regiments Stab 200 and Schützen Brigade 15's HQs. Things actually worsened during the not uncommon cases of friendly fire, when quick contact was badly needed. German troops had to revert to the obsolete system of pre-arranged smoke and flares signals to stop friendly artillery fire from pounding their own positions.

Intelligence

Lacking in most cases a real front line, the use of patrols and of prisoners as an intelligence source was strongly limited in North Africa. On the other hand, aerial reconnaissance and signal intelligence (sigint) provided many of the intelligence sources used by the Panzerarmee Afrika and the DAK. Aerial reconnaissance was the quickest and most immediate intelligence source. It was widely used since it could easily spot practically any moving vehicle, especially columns and large concentrations, though it faced some serious shortcomings. Firstly, because of the lack of land-to-air radio links, it was often very hard to distinguish whether such concentrations were friendly or enemy forces. Secondly, the large and extensive use of camouflage rendered vehicles visible only when moving, and the use of aerial reconnaissance was therefore limited only to battlefields. The only intelligence source capable of giving a deep, inside view of the enemy situation was sigint, in which Germans forces in North Africa excelled. The first signal intelligence unit to arrive in North Africa was the Horchzug (radio monitoring platoon) attached to the 5.leichte Division's 3.Kompanie/Nachrichten Abteilung 39. In late April 1941 this was absorbed into Oberleutnant (then Hauptmann) Alfred Seebohm's 3.Horchkompanie/

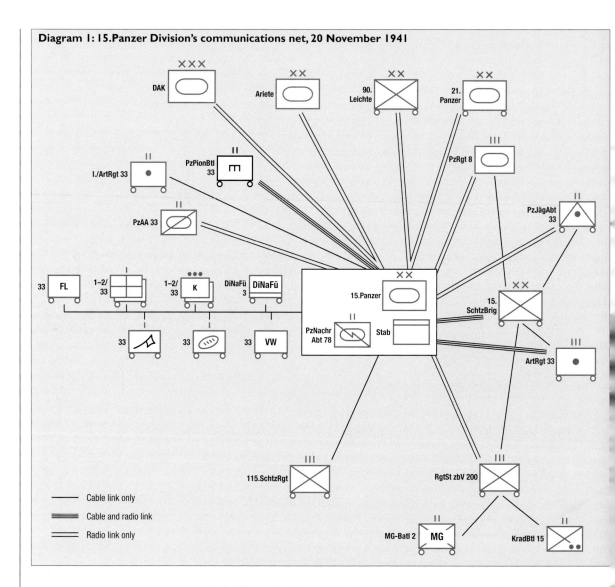

Diagram 1: 15.Panzer Division's communications net, 20 November 1941

Cable link only
Cable and radio link
Radio link only

Nachrichten Abteilung 56, itself a radio interception unit. One year later, in April 1942, this was eventually renamed Horchkompanie (mot) 621, most of which was eventually captured at Tell el Eisa on 10 July.

British carelessness in radio communications – particularly their use of simple codes easy to decipher – was of great help to German sigint. German sigint's first success came almost at once when, thanks to the information it supplied, Rommel was well aware there only were British rearguards at Mersa el Brega and, after he had started his drive into Cyrenaica, he quickly became aware they were withdrawing. In the months to follow, German sigint saw a series of ups and downs. Rommel's reaction to Operation *Battleaxe* in June 1941 was greatly helped by sigint, which informed him of the actual start date of the operation and also of British intentions during the battle. On the other hand, one of sigint's greatest failures was Operation *Crusader*, which came as a complete surprise. In the first half of 1942 a good deal of Rommel's successes were due to both his sigint's activity and to the information provided by the 'good source' – the deciphered messages sent by the American military attaché in Egypt. The fact that this intelligence source eventually run dry in July 1942, when most of Seebohm's Horchkompanie was also destroyed, certainly suggests that a good deal of Rommel's failures at El Alamein were due to the lack of intelligence.

Unit status

On 11 February 1941 the first German units landed at Tripoli. Rommel joined them the following day. On 14 February the first combat units of 5.leichte Division arrived, namely Panzer Aufklärungs Abteilung 3 and Panzerjäger Abteilung 39, and Rommel rushed both to the front line. One week later, on 21 February, the DAK was formed and Generalmajor Streich arrived to take over command of 5.leichte Division. Practically unhindered, transports continued to arrive in North Africa; by 25 February some 7,232 men, 2,366 vehicles and about 4,000 tons of supplies (both Wehrmacht and Luftwaffe) had arrived at Tripoli. By 10 March the figures had risen to 12,920 men, 4,074 vehicles and 10,560 tons of supplies. On 24 March Rommel attacked the British positions at El Agheila, and a week later his drive into Cyrenaica was started. The day before, 30 March, the first units of 15.Panzer Division began to arrive at Tripoli (I./Flak 18, soon followed by Panzerjäger Abteilung 33 and most of Kradschützen Bataillon 15). On 10/11 April the DAK attempted for the first time to take Tobruk, and a second assault followed on 14–18 April. Also, by then, a defence line had been established on the Egyptian border at Sollum and the Halfaya Pass. The third attempt to take Tobruk with an assault failed on 30 April–3 May at Ras el Mdauuar and, by 1 May, 33,549 men, 11,330 vehicles and 36,332 tons of supplies had arrived in Africa. A first British attempt to break out of the German defences at the Halfaya Pass was repulsed on 15–27 May (Operation *Brevity*), as was the second attempt on 15–17 June (Operation *Battleaxe*). In June, with DAK's initial order of battle practically complete, its strength had risen to about 33,500 (**Table 15**). It would be wrong, however, to assume that it was at full strength since the 1,500km drive to Tobruk and the hard battles that followed greatly reduced DAK's combat strength. Unfortunately complete data are not available, but two examples are worthwhile: on 13 April Panzer Regiment 5's actual strength consisted of four PzKpfw I (established strength was 25), 15 PzKpfw II (45), nine PzKpfw III (71) and nine PzKpfw IV (20). Panzer Regiment 8 was in no better shape with 28 PzKpfw II (45 on establishment), 26 PzKpfw III, 13 PzKpfw IV (99 on establishment) and five Befehlspanzer. On 14 April MG Bataillon 8's combat strength[2] was three officers, 21 NCOs and 92 other ranks. It is worth noting that British forces surrounded at Tobruk alone numbered about 29,000.

The Western Desert proved an even worse enemy; between March and June 1941 the DAK lost 12,203 men, but only 3,512 of them had been casualties the rest were sick. During summer and early autumn sickness increased DAK's losses while, between July and October, the number of battle casualties dropped. In October that eventually caused a sensible reduction of strength to the now Panzergruppe Afrika (formed on 15 August 1941), since most of those who were sick were sent back to Europe. On the other hand, the tank situation improved steadily. On 19 August Panzer Regiment 5 had 20 PzKpfw I, 30 PzKpfw II, 57 PzKpfw III and 16 PzKpfw IV (plus one captured Mark VI); Panzer Regiment 8 had 41 PzKpfw II, 70 PzKpfw III and 16 PzKpfw IV (plus six captured Mark II). (All data refers, unless otherwise stated, to serviceable

A 150mm schwere Feldhaubitze 13/1 (sfl) auf Geschützwagen Lorraine Schlepper (f) (SdKfz 135/1), one of the first German attempts to produce a self-propelled howitzer. Sixty-four examples of this type were built (plus 12 others armed with a 105mm howitzer) and in 1944 they formed the basis of 21.Panzer Division's artillery in Normandy. (Archivio Ufficio Storico Stato Maggiore Esercito)

2 *Gefechtsstärke*, that is combat unit's strength without trains (divisional combat strength summarizes the combat strength of all subordinated combat units).

Table 15: DAK – PzGruppe/PzAOK Afrika strength and losses, March 1941–November 1942

| | 1941 | | | | | | | | |
	March	April	May	June	July	Aug	Sept	Oct	Nov
Strength	14,500	19,000	30,000	33,500	42,000	46,000	48,500	48,500	38,000
Killed	24	158	267	131	18	45	61	11	473
Wounded	41	565	929	459	205	184	179	70	1,680
Missing	2	388	280	268	41	11	14	7	962
Total	67	1,111	1,476	858	264	240	254	88	3,115
Percentage of total strength	0.5	5.8	4.9	2.6	0.6	0.5	0.5	0.2	8.2
Sick	635	815	2,516	4,725	7,983	9,890	11,245	11,066	5,377
Percentage of total strength	4.4	4.3	8.4	14.0	19.0	21.5	23.2	22.8	14.2
Total losses	702	1,926	3,992	5,583	8,247	10,130	11,499	11,154	8,492

Note: Since many different methods were used to count strength, in some cases figures may not agree with those appearing elsewhere.

weapons.) Figures for 10 September were: Panzer Regiment 5, 13 PzKpfw I, 34 PzKpfw II, 60 PzKpfw III and 16 PzKpfw IV (plus one captured Mark VI); Panzer Regiment 8, 41 PzKpfw II, 64 PzKpfw III and 13 PzKpfw IV (plus two captured Mark II). Following 21.Panzer Division's dash to Sofafi on 14 September (Operation *Midsummer Night's Dream*), on 9 October actual tank strength changed as follows: Panzer Regiment 5, 13 PzKpfw I, 20 PzKpfw II, 55 PzKpfw III and 10 PzKpfw IV; Panzer Regiment 8, 42 PzKpfw II, 77 PzKpfw III and 18 PzKpfw IV. On the eve of Operation *Crusader* both Panzer divisions were still far from full strength, although they represented a powerful force. On 11 November 1941, 15.Panzer Division had a combat strength of 223 officers, 1,274 NCOs and 5,973 other ranks (ration strength, which includes the sick, was 335 officers, 2,004 NCOs and 9,796 other ranks). Its weapons inventory included: 315 light machine guns, 79 heavy machine guns, 32 light mortars, 23 heavy mortars, 74 Panzerbüchse 39 and 4 Panzerbüchse 41, 24 Pak 36/36 37mm, one captured anti-tank 40mm, 28 Pak 38 50mm, five light infantry guns, 24 light howitzers and 11 heavy howitzers. Panzer Regiment 8's tank strength on 19 November was: 38 PzKpfw II, 76 PzKpfw III, 21 PzKpfw IV and nine Befehlspanzer. On 15 November, 21.Panzer Division's combat strength was 203 officers, 1,257 NCOs and 5,512 other ranks (ration strength was 241 officers, 1,494 NCOs and 6,104 other ranks). Its weapons inventory included 576 light machine guns, 74 heavy machine guns, 21 light mortars, 18 heavy mortars, 91 Panzerbüchse, ten light infantry guns, two heavy infantry guns, 30 37mm Pak 35/36, 45 50mm Pak 38, 12 light howitzers and 32 20mm Flak 38. Panzer Regiment 5's tank strength on 17 November 1941 included 35 PzKpfw II, 68 PzKpfw III, 17 PzKpfw IV and four Befehlspanzer. In mid-November 1941, 90.leichte Afrika Division's actual strength, including several attachments (9./Schützen Regiment 104, 2./Panzer Pionier 200, Aufklärungs Abteilung 3 and 33, II./Artillerie Regiment 155, two *Flak Abteilungen* and one *Heeres Küsten Artillerie Abteilung* plus a single battery) was 352 officers, 2,017 NCOs and 9,709 other ranks, though it actually dropped to about 248 officers, 1,461 NCOs and 7,310 other ranks without attachments. Weapons inventory (attached units excluded) included at least 412 light and 46 heavy MGs, 91 Panzerbüchse, 48 heavy mortars, 15 infantry guns, eight light guns and 27 Panzerjäger I.

Operation *Crusader*, launched on 18 November 1941, was the very first big battle that saw the entire DAK involved. On 5 December Rommel eventually decided to withdraw back to El Agheila, a march that was completed by 12 January 1942 putting thus an end to what the Germans called the *Winterschlacht*, the 'winter battle'. Its consequences were appalling: up to the

| | 1942 | | | | | | | | | | |
Dec	Jan	Feb	March	Apr	May	June	July	Aug	Sept	Oct	Nov
32,000	31,000	33,000	36,000	39,000	43,000	40,000	48,000	57,000	54,000	52,000	41,000
446	112	41	11	20	278	845	796	114	376	422	505
1,640	326	175	67	120	1044	3318	3193	601	1485	1,263	1,500
3,081	526	10	175	6	356	473	1,167	43	214	2,240	3,417
5,167	964	226	253	146	1,678	4,636	5,156	758	2,075	3,925	5,422
16.1	3.1	0.7	0.7	0.4	3.9	11.6	10.7	1.3	3.8	7.5	13.2
2,998	3,077	2,635	3,781	3,867	5,767	3,323	5,051	9,418	11,054	9,954	5,860
9.4	9.9	8.0	10.5	9.9	13.4	8.3	10.5	16.5	20.5	19.1	14.3
8,165	4,041	2,861	4,034	4,013	7,445	7,959	10,207	10,176	13,129	13,879	11,282

end of December 1941 the DAK had lost 42 PzKpfw II, 135 PzKpfw III, 34 PzKpfw IV, 18 Befehlspanzer, 46 armoured cars, 383 cars, 483 lorries, 203 tractors, 122 motorcycles, more than 1,000 light weapons (411 pistols, 145 MPs, 735 rifles and carbines), 127 light MGs, 27 Panzerbüchse, five Panzerbüchse 41, 29 37mm Pak 35/36, 13 Panzerjäger I, 17 50mm Pak 38, 56 light mortars, 46 heavy mortars, 19 light howitzers, eight heavy howitzers, six heavy 100mm guns, one heavy 210mm mortar, 23 20mm Flak 38 and 13 heavy 88mm Flak. Most of these losses occurred during the 'winter battle': 95 PzKpfw III (out of the 144 available in mid-November), 25 PzKpfw IV (out of 38), 25 armoured cars (out of 32), 16 light and eight heavy howitzers. On 12 December 1941 Panzer Regiment 5's tank strength was seven PzKpfw II, nine PzKpfw III and two PzKpfw IV. Panzer Regiment 8 had eight PzKpfw II, 22 PzKpfw III and three PzKpfw IV. Personnel also suffered heavily; in spite of a considerable reduction in cases of sickness (in November 1941 figures were half than the previous month), which eventually lasted until April 1941, battle casualties figures rose sharply. Losses in November–December amounted to more than half of the total losses suffered between March and December 1941; these included 919 killed out of 1,634, 3,320 wounded out of 5,952 and 4,043 missing out of 5,054. The desert also added its own burden for, by January 1942, the DAK had lost about 50–60 per cent of its lorries, only partly due to enemy action. Divisional strengths and weaponry suffered accordingly: by 21 December 1941 15.Panzer Division's combat strength was down to 163 officers, 704 NCOs and 3,251 other ranks (ration strength was 243 officers, 1,297 NCOs and 6,128 other ranks). Its weapons inventory included now 161 light and 36 heavy MGs, seven light and 12 heavy mortars, 37 Panzerbüchse 39, two Panzerbüchse 41, 10 37mm Pak 35/36, 27 50mm Pak 38, three light infantry guns, 12 light and five heavy howitzer, six PzKpfw II, 12 PzKpfw III, one PzKpfw IV and one Befehlspanzer. On 15 December 21.Panzer's combat strength was 142 officers, 694 NCOs and 3,517 other ranks (ration strength 179 officers, 1,170 NCOs and 4,570 other ranks), while weapons included 216 light and 31 heavy MGs, three light and 11 heavy mortars, 19 Panzerbüchse, five light and two heavy infantry guns, eight 37mm Pak 35/36, 30 50mm Pak 38, seven light and four heavy howitzers and 25 20mm Flak 38. 90.leichte Division's actual strength is hard to assess, but on 29 December it seems to have had about 2,000 men, 177 light and 29 heavy MGs, 12 heavy mortars, 39 Panzerbüchse, 54 guns (either Pak or artillery), 20 Flak guns and 14 Panzerjäger I.

On 5 January 1942, for the first time in months, a convoy arrived at Tripoli carrying badly needed reinforcements for the DAK: amongst others 54 tanks, 19 armoured cars and more than 3,500 tons of supplies. Many others would

A column of PzKpfw II Ausf. Cs belonging to 15.Panzer Division's Panzer Regiment 5 races across the desert. Note in the background the column of wheeled vehicles that includes (first from right) a captured light lorry. The use of a single number on the tank's turret probably denotes the regimental leichte Panzerzug. (Carlo Pecchi Collection)

have licked their wounds and reorganized their units. Rommel did not and he showed that the DAK had been beaten, but not defeated. A reorganization did in fact take place and by 18 January DAK's tank strength included 97 serviceable Panzers (22 PzKpfw II, 66 PzKpfw III and nine PzKpfw IV) plus 14 others in short-term repair and 28 arriving. By 20 January DAK's tank strength was 121 serviceable Panzers. On 21 January 1942 Rommel attacked again, completely thwarting both his enemies and his superiors, and by 5 February western Cyrenaica had been reconquered, this time at a cheap price: Kampfgruppe Marcks, DAK's leading force, lost only one dead and 13 wounded (the DAK lost five killed, ten wounded and 25 missing). Even its tank strength was only slightly reduced at the end of the campaign (on 3 February DAK's tank inventory included 27 PzKpfw II, 65 PzKpfw III, ten PzKpfw IV and four Befehlspanzer). The period of calm that followed, with both armies facing each other on the Gazala Line, enabled the DAK to rest, reorganize, refit and retrain. Thanks to the heavy air attacks against Malta, reinforcements and supplies reached North Africa in greater quantities. On 11 March 1942, 15.Panzer Division's combat strength was 197 officers, 921 NCOs and 3,997 other ranks (rations strength was 264 officers, 1,423 NCOs and 6,291 other ranks). Weapons inventory included 256 light and 55 heavy MGs, 7 light and 15 heavy mortars, five light infantry guns, 42 light and four heavy Panzerbüchsen, 15 37mm Pak 35/36, 36 50mm Pak 38, two captured 40mm anti-tank guns, 15 light and five heavy howitzers, 18 PzKpfw II, 71 PzKpfw III, eight PzKpfw IV, one Befehlspanzer and 10 20mm Flak 38. 21.Panzer Division's strength on 21 March 1942 was 200 officers, 879 NCOs and 3,997 other ranks (ration strength was 226 officers, 1,058 NCOs and 4,601 other ranks). On 15 March the division had 357 light and 36 heavy MGs, 12 heavy mortars, 38 Panzerbüchsen, five light and one heavy infantry gun, 11 37mm Pak 35/36, 29 50mm Pak 38, four captured 40mm anti-tanks, 18 light and eight heavy howitzers, and four captured 25-pdrs. Tank strength included seven PzKpfw II, 39 PzKpfw III, six PzKpfw IV and three Befehlspanzer. 90.leichte's actual strength on 15 March 1942 was 171 officers, 875 NCOs and 4,157 other ranks. Weapons inventory as of 18 March included 172 light and 21 heavy MGs, 15 heavy mortars, 37 light and 11 heavy Panzerbüchsen, 33 37mm Pak 35/36, 12 50mm Pak 38, 26 Russian 76.2mm anti-tank guns, 11 Flak 38, six self-propelled sIG 33 and eight Dianas.

Panzerarmee Afrika's strength rose steadily until May, when it matched DAK's strength of the previous July. Actual strengths before Operation *Theseus*, the attack on the Gazala Line, were far from the established ones, yet the overall situation was quite good. 15. Panzer Division's combat strength on 21 May 1942 was 228 officers, 1,157 NCOs and 4,795 other ranks (rations strength was 291 officers, 1,676 NCOs and 7,037 other ranks). Weapons included 286 light and 26 heavy MGs, one light and 26 heavy mortars, 35 light and four heavy Panzerbüchsen, two light infantry guns, 16 37mm Pak 35/36, 46 50mm Pak 38, one captured 40mm anti-tank gun, 23 light and eight heavy howitzers, four 100mm guns, three heavy 210mm mortars and 14 20mm Flak 38. Panzer strength was 24 PzKpfw II, 111 PzKpfw III, 20 PzKpfw IV and two Befehlspanzer. Though impressive, these figures do not reveal the actual situation when compared to established strengths: Schützen Regiment 115's strength was at 60 per cent of the establishment (vehicles were at 45 per cent), Panzer Aufklärungs Abteilung 33 had 85 per cent of its established personnel and 70 per cent of vehicles. Artillerie Regiment 33 only had two-thirds of its equipment and 70 per cent of established personnel, while Panzer Pionier Bataillon 33 only had 60 per cent of its personnel, 50 per cent of vehicles and only 20 per cent of its engineering equipment. Divisions Nachschub Führer 33 was in even poorer condition: only 70 lorries were serviceable, 35 per cent of the establishment, and it was remarked that heavy losses had to be expected. 21.Panzer Division's combat strength was slightly inferior to that of its sister division, as it had 241 officers, 1,028 NCOs and 4,453 other ranks (rations strength was 272 officers, 1,270 NCOs and 5,211 other ranks). Its actual weapons' strength is unknown, though the number of Panzers can be reconstructed: it included 29 PzKpfw II, 126 PzKpfw III and 18 PzKpfw IV, for a total of 53 PzKpfw II, 242 PzKpfw III (including five with the Panzerarmee) and 38 PzKpfw IV. According to some sources, 18 PzKpfw III were armed with the long barrelled Kwk 38 L/42. Here too, percentages of actual strength versus established strength reveal a grim reality: though Panzer Regiment 5 had 89 per cent of its established strength, Schützen Regiment 104 was only at 58 per cent. The situation was no better with other units: Artillerie Regiment 155 was at 78 per cent, Panzerjäger Abteilung 39 at 69 per cent and only Pionier Bataillon 200 was close to full strength with 90 per cent of its established strength. 90.leichte Infanterie Division's strength on 15 May was 277 officers, 1,467 NCOs and 7,279 other ranks. Weapons included (data incomplete) 157 light and 44 heavy MGs, 21 heavy mortars, 14 heavy Panzerbüchsen, 13 37mm Pak 36/36, 15 (eventually 40) 50mm Pak 38, 32 Russian 76.2mm Pak 36(r), 17 Panzerjäger I, seven Dianas, three Sturmgeschütze, eight armoured cars, 25 20mm Flak 38, 28 Russian 76.2mm guns, four captured 25-pdrs, 12 self-propelled sIG 33 and two 88mm Flak 18s In May 1942 DAK's divisions only included some 58 per cent of its total strength (25,000 out of 43,000). The real divisional slice was even worse, since only about 50 per cent of the whole Panzerarmee's strength was made of combat troops, the rest consisting of supply troops and services (figures matching those of the entire German Army in June 1942).

The attack against the Gazala Line started on 26 May 1942 and soon turned into a major battle that, by 17 June, had ended in favour of the Germans . Apparently, German units did not suffer much from the battle: on 1 June, 21.Panzer Division's combat strength was 241 officers, 919 NCOs and 5,566 other ranks. By 11 June it was only slightly reduced with 228 officers, 871 NCOs and 4,428 other ranks (rations strength was 280 officers, 1,137 NCOs and 6,063 other ranks). On 17 June the division had eight PzKpfw II (plus two in short-term repair), 26 PzKpfw III (plus four in repair), eight PzKpfw III Sp (*Spezial*, long barrelled) (plus one), two PzKpfw IV (plus one in repair) and two PzKpfw IV Sp. Actually, from 25 May the DAK started to receive good quantities of both PzKpfw III and PzKpfw IV Sp, up to 90 and 20 respectively, though most of them began to arrive in July and August. On 7–9 June 1942 DAK's combat strength included 80 Panzers with Panzer Regiment 5

Captured British vehicles were largely used by the DAK, first because of the widespread shortage of motor transport but also because they were actually better suited for the desert than the German ones. A Morris commercial lorry pressed into German service; unit insignias have been censored, but 15.Panzer Division's one can still be seen on the right mudguard. (Carlo Pecchi Collection)

plus another 32 with Panzer Regiment 8, 947 men with Schützen Regiment 104 (42 per cent of the establishment) and 667 with I. and III./Schützen Regiment 115 (35 per cent of established strength, II./SR 115 had been disbanded). 90.leichte Division's strength included (motorized units only) 425 men with Schützen Regiment 155, 14 Pak 38 with Panzerjäger Abteilung 190 and six Panzerjäger I plus four Dianas with Panzerjäger Abteilung 605. On 11 June DAK's Panzer strength was 25 PzKpfw II, 83 PzKpfw III, 27 PzKpfw III Sp, eight PzKpfw IV and six PzKpfw IV Sp – all in all, still a powerful force. Having broken his enemy, on 18 June Rommel prepared the assault against Tobruk, which eventually fell on 20–21 June. At this point he took the fateful decision to continue to advance into Egypt, a decision certainly taken in part thanks to DAK's actual strengths, still relatively good, and to the huge amount of booty captured at Tobruk.

Panzerarmee Afrika crossed the Egyptian border on 23 June and for the next two days advanced to Mersa Matruh, which was seized on the 28th. Two days later the Panzerarmee was in sight of the El Alamein line. Scant data exists for this period, but some examples are quite revealing. Panzer Regiment 5's tank strength on 23 June was 11 PzKpfw II, 21 PzKpfw III and six PzKpfw III Sp; one week later, on 30 June, it was two PzKpfw II, 19 PzKpfw IIs, six PzKpfw III Sp and one PzKpfw IV. On 29 June 90.leichte Division's total strength was 1,929 all ranks, and its weapons included 14 50mm Pak 38 with Panzerjäger Abteilung 190, five Russian 76.2mm guns and four captured 25-pdrs. On 1 July 21.Panzer Division's combat strength was 188 officers, 786 NCOs and 3,842 other ranks (rations strength was 227 officers, 1,179 NCOs and 5,334 other ranks). Apparently that was enough to attack, which the Panzerarmee actually did on 1 July, thus starting the first battle of Alamein that ended on the 27th, a German failure that brought the DAK close to collapse. Facing unexpected resistance the already worn-out DAK suffered heavy losses, which reduced its already weak strength to the barest minimum. The Panzers, however, were not the ones to suffer the most. On 6 July Panzer Regiment 5 tank strength still included four PzKpfw II, 13 PzKpfw III, seven PzKpfw III Sp, one PzKpfw IV and one PzKpfw IV Sp, and it even increased by 9 July, reaching some 17 PzKpfw III and eight PzKpfw III Sp. On the other hand, on 8 July Panzer Regiment 8 was in a rather bad shape having only one PzKpfw II, 11 PzKpfw III and one PzKpfw IV. However, by 14 July Panzer Regiment 5's tank strength was still relatively intact with two PzKpfw II, 13 PzKpfw III, six PzKpfw III Sp and one PzKpfw IV, though it eventually dropped by 22 July when it was left with only four PzKpfw II, 12 PzKpfw III, five PzKpfw III Sp and one PzKpfw IV. Panzerarmee's tank strength on 21 July was six PzKpfw II, 27 PzKpfw III, six PzKpfw III Sp, one PzKpfw IV and two PzKpfw IV Sp, with some 100 other tanks under repair. Yet, losses were soon recouped, and by 25 July Panzer Regiment 5's strength included four PzKpfw II, 16 PzKpfw III, seven PzKpfw III Sp and two PzKpfw IV Sp. On 27 July Panzerarmee's tank strength included 47 PzKpfw III, 16 PzKpfw III Sp, four PzKpfw IV and 9 PzKpfw IV Sp. The infantry suffered the most, as its losses could not easily be recouped. On 8 July DAK's strength still included 50 Panzers, 15 armoured cars, 20 armoured AFVs, 27 gun batteries, 26 88mm Flak 35/36 and 65 20mm Flak 38. But, in the meantime, the strength of both Schützen Regiment 104 and 115 was only 300 each (Schützen Regiment 115 was left with two companies each 80 strong, plus the cadres of its III.Bataillon), while 90.leichte Division's four regiments (Sonderverband 288 included) only had about 1,500 men (the entire division was no more than 2,200 strong). On 4 July 21.Panzer Division assessed that while its weapons-oriented units still possessed good percentages of their established strength (Panzer Regiment 5 had 63 per cent, Artillerie Regiment 155 had even increased with respect to the previous May, up to 83 per cent, while Panzerjäger Abteilung 39 was almost unchanged with 67 per cent), its Schützen Regiment 104 had dropped to 37 per cent. On 21 July Panzerarmee Afrika estimated that only 30 per cent of its personnel strength was left, along with 15 per cent of its Panzer strength, 70 per cent of its artillery strength, 40 per cent of its anti-tank gun strength and 50 per cent of its heavy Flak strength. In fact, 15.Panzer Division's Panzer Regiment 8 only had four PzKpfw II and 14 PzKpfw III while its Panzergrenadier Regiment 115 had a combat strength of 946 all ranks, with the divisional combat strength at 2,415 all ranks. Panzer Regiment 5's tank strength included 15 PzKpfw III and five PzKpfw III Sp though Panzergrenadier Regiment 104 had a combat strength of 591 all ranks (divisional combat strength was 2,409). 90.leichte Afrika Division's overall strength was 3,337.

Understandably, Rommel's first concern was to recover Panzerarmee Afrika's infantry strength, which could only be done by getting hold of reinforcements. From July 1942 both 164.leichte Afrika Division and the Ramcke Fallschirmjäger Brigade's personnel began to arrive in North Africa by airlift, while vehicles and heavy equipment were brought in by ship. The airlift had started in April, but until June 1942 only 22,912 men (plus 6,645 Lufwaffe personnel) were transported. Figures increased sharply between July and August 1942, when some 24,606 Wehrmacht and 11,620 Luftwaffe personnel were airlifted to North Africa. Such a dramatic arrival of new men had grave consequences. Although Panzerarmee Afrika's strength had risen to 57,000 by August 1942, sickness also rose dramatically between July and September eventually curtailing its strength by 20 per cent (**Table 15**). A recovery took place, however, and by mid-August Panzerarmee Afrika was back up to a reasonable strength: according to its estimates it had 75 per cent of its established personnel, 50 per cent of its Panzers, 85 per cent of its artillery, 60 per cent of its Paks and 70 per cent of its heavy Flaks. On 15 August 15.Panzer Division's combat strength was 6,938 all ranks, and its tank inventory included 15 PzKpfw II, 51 PzKpfw III, 29 PzKpfw III Sp, three PzKpfw IV and eight PzKpfw IV Sp. 21.Panzer Division's combat strength on 20 August was 253 officers, 1,044 NCOs and 5,173 other ranks (rations strength was 307 officers, 1,475 NCOs and 6,730 other ranks), and it had 12 PzKpfw II, 46 PzKpfw III, 33 PzKpfw III Sp, five PzKpfw IV and 12 PzKpfw IV Sp. On the same day, 90.leichte Afrika Division's total strength included 275 officers, 1,211 NCOs and 6,763 other ranks. 164.leichte Afrika Division, still arriving, had a combat strength of 8,293, Aufklärungs Abteilung 220 excluded. On the eve of the battle of Alam Halfa on 30 August, DAK's tank inventory included 93 PzKpfw III, 73 PzKpfw III Sp, 10 PzKpfw IV and 27 PzKpfw IV Sp. The battle of Alam Halfa, fought between 30 August and 6 September 1942, ended in a

Bringing supplies to the front was one of DAK's greatest problems, especially during its advance into Egypt in 1942. With most of the supplies unloaded at Tripoli and given the lack of any railway, the Germans had to rely almost exclusively on motor transport, which in turn also meant consuming a large quantity of fuel to take the rest to the front. An Opel 'Blitz' lorry is being loaded; to the right an Auto Union/Horch staff car. (Carlo Pecchi Collection)

failure but it did not cost DAK too dearly: overall German losses included 1,859 all ranks, of which 386 were killed, and also 38 Panzers and armoured cars. By 21 September 21.Panzer Division's combat strength was 218 officers, 1,121 NCOs and 5,409 other ranks (rations strength was 271 officers, 1,395 NCOs and 6,552 other ranks). On 15 September Panzer Regiment 5 still had 19 PzKpfw II, 38 PzKpfw III, 35 PzKpfw III Sp, five PzKpfw IV and 11 PzKpfw IV Sp. 90.leichte Afrika Division seems to have suffered more since, on 21 September, its combat strength was 143 officers, 555 NCOs and 2,882 other ranks (rations strength was of 157 officers, 722 NCOs and 3,563 other ranks).

Once more Panzergruppe Afrika recovered, this time getting ready for the unavoidable enemy offensive which, as everybody knew, would be launched with overwhelming resources. On 20 October 1942 Panzergruppe Afrika combat units' rations strength was 48,854, with the following breakdown: 15.Panzer Division 9,368, 21.Panzer Division 9,517, 90.leichte Afrika Division 6,269, 164.leichte Afrika Division 9,623, 19.Flak Division der Luftwaffe 6,302, Luftwaffe Jäger Brigade 1 (formerly the Ramcke Brigade) 4,706, Höhere Artillerie Kommandeur Afrika 3,069. Actual infantry combat strength was 12,147, mostly with 164.Division (5,076) and the Luftwaffe Jäger Brigade (2,380). Panzergrenadier Regiment 104's combat strength was 1,792, while Panzergrenadier Regiment 115's was 1,393. Tank strength included 12 PzKpfw II, 38 PzKpfw III, 43 PzKpfw III Sp, two PzKpfw IV and 15 PzKpfw IV Sp with Panzer Regiment 8, plus another 18 PzKpfw II, 43 PzKpfw III, 43 PzKpfw III Sp, six PzKpfw IV and 15 PzKpfw IV Sp with Panzer Regiment 5. The British offensive at El Alamein started on 23 October, and the battle eventually ended on 4 November 1942 with Rommel's decision to withdraw, which marked the first, real defeat of the DAK. By 26 October Panzer Regiment 8's tank strength was down to eight PzKpfw II, 16 PzKpfw III, 16 PzKpfw III Sp, one PzKpfw IV and six PzKpfw IV Sp. It decreased steadily until the end of October (on the 30th it was six PzKpfw II, 11 PzKpfw III, 15 PzKpfw III Sp, one PzKpfw IV and four PzKpfw IV Sp), until Operation *Supercharge* was launched. On 4 November Panzer Regiment 8's tank strength was three PzKpfw III, one PzKpfw III Sp, one PzKpfw IV and one PzKpfw IV Sp. By 8 November it no longer possessed a single Panzer. On 18 November DAK's strength, inclusive of both 15. and 21.Panzer Divisions, was 17,767 (15.Panzer Division's combat strength on 21 November was 1,125, its rations strength 6,923). Army, corps and supply troops added 14,650 more. DAK's weapons inventory included 541 MGs, 14 mortars, 12 Paks, 35 Panzers, 16 armoured cars and 14 various guns. 90.leichte Afrika Division's strength was 5,118 (the division had 322 MGs, 22 mortars, 31 Paks, four armoured cars and seven guns). 164.leichte Afrika Division's strength was 4,935 (the division only had 127 MGs, 30 mortars and two Paks). The long road back had begun.

Marching in the desert; a column of an unknown *Panzerjäger Abteilung* (tactical symbol barely visible on the left mudguard) keeps moving. In the foreground a Demag D7 SdKfz 10 halftrack is towing a Pak 38 50mm gun, in the background a captured British Morris commercial lorry. The shadows and the fact that the soldiers are still wrapped up in their overcoats suggest the photo was taken at sunrise. (Carlo Pecchi Collection)

Lessons learned

In a similar way to its campaigns of 1941–42, the image of the DAK has many lights and shadows. Rommel's brilliant leadership, superior German tactics and an overall asset proportionally better than the rest of the German Army made early successes possible – principally the first drive into Cyrenaica and the defence of the Sollum–Halfaya line. On the other hand lack of experience and incomplete training, as well as inadequate weaponry and equipment, especially compared to those available to DAK's enemies, ultimately provided the backdrop to early defeats at Tobruk and during Operation *Crusader*. Experience gained was not, however, wasted and in 1942 many changes were introduced. Training was improved, taking advantage of experienced personnel, and the combination of both adequate training and experience gained eventually emphasized German tactical superiority. Unit organization was altered, making good many shortcomings; in 1941 German units greatly suffered from their unbalanced organization, which saw three different divisional assets none of which was actually suitable for the Western Desert. Changes introduced in September 1941, though useful, were only a provisional remedy, but those introduced in April 1942 brought many decisive innovations. DAK's divisions were now well balanced and, thanks to a larger weapons allotment and to the introduction of new and more powerful weapons, they turned into extremely powerful and successful units. Not that every shortcoming had been eliminated: a lack of motor vehicles, especially suitable ones, could only be made good thanks to the large amount of captured enemy equipment. Also the new divisional organization, based on the principle of 'more weapons, less men', coupled with strengths perpetually below establishment, eventually imposed too severe a strain on the relatively few available men. The result was that when the Alamein Line was reached, the DAK had to face a simple reality: it had gone beyond its limits.

A column belonging to a Panzer division's *Nachrichten Abteilung*, very likely portrayed in spring or summer 1941. The first vehicle is an eight-wheeled Panzerfunkwagen SdKfz 263 followed by a BMW combination and by two kleiner Panzerfunkwagen SdKfz 260/261. The DAK's 'palm with swastika' insignia stands out on the dark-grey background. (Carlo Pecchi Collection)

Nevertheless, the fact remains that the stunning victories of May–June 1942, obtained against a superior enemy, were the result of a decisive evolution that, in a few months, brought the DAK to remarkable levels of capability and efficiency. As a matter of fact, had the DAK seized Tobruk in 1941 we may very likely suppose that given its then lack of experience, its faulty organization and all other shortcomings, it might not have been able to continue with its offensive into Egypt, at least successfully. And that was not just a matter of weapons and equipment: some of DAK's most stunning successes were achieved when it faced a superior enemy and before modern and powerful weapons became available in quantity. Both drives into Cyrenaica were conducted with scarce resources: the defence against Operations *Brevity* and *Battleaxe* was successful thanks to the ingenious use of the 88mm and the victories of May–June 1942 were obtained before large quantities of the newest, most powerful, tanks were available. It is once more a matter of light and shadow. In October 1942 the DAK was in comparison stronger and much more skilled than it had been in 1941, yet it was finally defeated because its own doctrines and tactics had to be surrendered in favour of those imposed by its enemy. At the very end, neither weapons nor experience could assure success on the battlefield, though they certainly influenced defeats.

What then were the real secrets of the DAK, those that made possible its many successes? Rommel was certainly one; no matter whether his strategic and tactical skills can be criticized or not, the fact remains that his personality, his brilliant leadership and his capability to face changing situations proved decisive in many cases. Also, one should not forget that his subordinates, as well as most of the DAK's senior and junior officers, possessed remarkable skills, and leadership capabilities. Undoubtedly, it was thanks to the combination of these two factors that the DAK became such a solid, strong and welded group and, in spite of its shortcomings, such a successful fighting force. Beyond any doubt, this is the true lesson that should be learnt from the history of the Deutsches Afrika Korps. Ingenuity, skills, leadership, capability to face changing situations and to react appropriately were the qualities that made Rommel, his subordinate commanders and most of the DAK's men capable of dealing with a hostile environment and a superior enemy.

Two DAK soldiers taking a smoke break outside their PzKpfw III during a moment of calm. In spite of strict regulations concerning uniforms, soldiers at the front had a more relaxed attitude and often took advantage of non-regulation but otherwise comfortable items. (Carlo Pecchi Collection)

Bibliography

This work is mainly based on primary sources collected both at the Bundesarchiv-Militärarchiv (Freiburg im Breisgau, Germany) and at the National Archives and Records Administration (College Park, Maryland, USA). In particular the following have been used: Oberkommando des Heeres/Generalstab des Heeres records (BA-MA, RH 2 collection), Panzergruppe/Panzerarmee Afrika records (BA-MA RH 19 VIII collection. NARA microfilm publication T-313), Deutsches Afrika Korps records (NARA microfilm publication T-314), 15.Panzer Division, 21.Panzer Division, 90.leichte Afrika Division and 164.leichte Afrika Division records (NARA microfilm publication T-315). The list of publications about the war in North Africa, the Afrika Korps and Rommel is huge, and the following is only a short summary. Interested readers may consult Colin F. Baxter's *The War in North Africa, 1940–1943: A Selected Bibliography* (Westport, CT: Greenwood Press, 1996) for further reading.

Aberger, Heinz-Dietrich, *Die 5. (lei.)/21. Panzer Division in Nordafrika, 1941–1943* (Reutlingen: Preussischer Militär-Verlag, 1994)

Agar-Hamilton, J.A.I., and Turner, L., *Crisis in the Desert, May to July 1942* (South African Armed Forces in the Second World War) (Cape Town: Oxford University Press, 1952)

Agar-Hamilton, J.A.I., and Turner, L., *The Sidi Rezegh Battles, 1941* (South African Armed Forces in the Second World War) (Cape Town: Oxford University Press, 1957)

Barnett, Correlli, *Hitler's Generals* (New York: Weidenfeld, 1989)

Behrendt, Hans-Otto, *Rommel's Intelligence in the Desert Campaign* (London: William Kimber, 1985)

Bender, Roger James, and Law, Richard D., *Uniforms, Organization and History of the Afrikakorps* (Mountain View, CA: Bender, 1973)

Bharucha, P.C., *North African Campaign, 1940–1943* (Official History of the Indian Armed Forces in the Second World War) (Delhi: Combined Inter-Services Historical Centre, 1956)

Boog, Horst, Rahn, Werner, Stumpf, Reinhard, and Wegner, Bernd, *Das Deutsche Reich und der Zweite Band 6: Der Globale Krieg. Die Ausweitung zum Weltkrieg und der Wechsel der Initiative 1941-1943* (Stuttgart: DVA, 1990)

Citino, Robert M. *Blitzkrieg to Desert Storm. The Evolution of Operational Warfare* (Lawrence, KS: University Press of Kansas, 2004)

Cooper, Matthew, and Lucas, James, *Panzer: The Armoured Force of the Third Reich* (London: Book Club, 1979)

Edwards, Roger, *Panzer: A Revolution in Warfare, 1939–1945* (London: Arms and Armour Press, 1989)

Forty, George, *Afrika Korps at War. Volume 1: The Road to Alexandria* (London: Ian Allan, 1978)

Fraser, David, *Knight's Cross. A Life of Field Marshal Erwin Rommel* (New York: Harper Collins, 1993)

Greene, Jack.,Massignani, Alessandro. *Rommel's North African Campaign. September 1940–November 1942* (Conshohocken, PA: Combined Books, 1994)

Hahn, Fritz, *Waffen und Geheimwaffen des deutschen Heeres, 1933-1945* (Bonn: Bernard & Graefe, 1998)

Irving, David, *The Trail of the Fox* (New York: Dutton, 1977)

Jörgensen, Christer, *Rommel's Panzer: Rommel and the Panzer Forces of the Blitzkrieg 1940–1942* (London: Brown Reference Group, 2003)

Law, Richard D., and Luther, Craig W.H., *Rommel. A Narrative and Pictorial History* (Mountain View, CA: Bender, 1980)

Lewin, Ronald, *The Life and Death of the Afrika Korps* (Barnsley: Pen & Sword, 2003)

Lewin, Ronald, *Rommel as Military Commander* (Barnsley: Pen & Sword, 2004)

Long, Gavin, *To Benghazi* (Australia in the War of 1939–1945, Series I, Volume I) (Canberra: Australian War Memorial, 1961)

Lucas, James, *Panzer Army Africa* (Abingdon: Purnell, 1977)

Macksey, Kenneth, *Afrika Korps* (Ballantine's Illustrated History of WWII) (New York: Ballantine, 1968)

Maughan, Barton, *Tobruk and el Alamein* (Australia in the War of 1939–1945, Series I, Volume III) (Canberra: Australian War Memorial, 1966)

Murphy, W.E., *The Relief of Tobruk* (Official History of New Zealand in the Second World War, 1939–45) (Wellington: War History Branch, 1961)

Nafziger, George F,. *Afrika Korps: An Organizational History, 1941–1943* (Pisgah, OH: Nafziger Collection, 1997)

Playfair, Ian Stanley Ord, *The Mediterranean and the Middle East, Volume 2: The Germans Come to the Help of Their Ally, 1941* (London: HMSO, 1956)

Playfair, Ian Stanley Ord, *The Mediterranean and the Middle East, Volume 3: British Fortunes Reach Their Lowest Ebb* (London: HMSO, 1960)

Rommel, Erwin, *The Rommel Papers* (London: Collins, 1953)

Rosado, Jorge, and Bishop, Chris, *German Wehrmacht Panzer Divisions 1939–45* (Staplehurst: Spellmount, 2005)

Schreiber, Gerhard, Stegemann, Bernd, and Vogel, Detlef, *Das Deutsche Reich und der Zweite Weltkrieg Band 3: Der Mittelmeerraum und Südosteuropa. Von der "non belligeranza" Italiens bis zum Kriegseintritt der Vereinigten Staaten* (Stuttgart: DVA, 1984)

Scoullar, Lt. Col. J.L., *Battle of Egypt: the Summer of 1942* (Official History of New Zealand in the Second World War, 1939–45) (Wellington: War History Branch, 1955)

Stolfi, R.H.S., *German Panzers on the Offensive. Russian Front – North Africa, 1941–1942* (Atglen, PA: Schiffer, 2003)

Stoves, Rolf, *Die gepanzerten und motorisierten deutschen Großverbände 1935–1945* (Eggolsheim: Nebel, n.d.)

Taysen, Adalbert von, *Tobruk 1941. Der Kampf in Nordafrika* (Freiburg: Rombach, 1976)

Toppe, Alfred, *Desert Warfare. German Experiences in World War II* (Historical Division, USAEUR, MS P-129, 1952)

Walker, Ronald, *Alam Halfa and el Alamein* (Official History of New Zealand in the Second World War, 1939–45) (Wellington: War History Branch, 1967)

Abbreviations and glossary

AA = *Aufklärungs Abteilung* (reconnaissance unit)

Abt = *Abteilung* (detachment, battalion)

AR = *Artillerie Regiment* (artillery regiment)

ArKo = *Artillerie Kommandeur* (artillery commander)

Art = *Artillerie* (Artillery)

Aufkl = *Aufklärung* (reconnaissance)

Ausf = *Ausführung* (variant)

Bäckerei = bakery

Bau = construction

Befh = *Befehl* (command), *Befehlshaber* (commander)

BefhSt = *Befehls Staffel* (command detachment)

Beob, Bb = *Beobachtungs* (observation)

Betr.Stoff = *Betriebs Stoff* (petrol)

Beute = captured

Bodenständig = static

Brig = brigade

Btl, Batl = *Bataillon* (battalion)

Bt, Bttr = *Batterie* (battery)

DAK = Deusches Afrika Korps (German Africa Corps)

DiNaFü = *Divisions Nachschub Führer* (divisional commander of supply units)

Div = *Division, Divisions* (division, divisional)

Drückerei = printing

DVA = *Divisions Verpflegungs Amt* (divisional food supply office)

Ersatzteil = spare part

FE = *Feld Ersatz* (field replacement)

Feldgendarmerie = military police

Feldlazarett = field hospital

Feldpost = field post

FH = *Feld Haubitze* (field howitzer)

Filtergerät = filter apparatus

FJ = *Fallschirmjäger* (paratrooper)

FJR = *Fallschirmjäger Regiment* (parachute regiment)

Fla = *Flieger Abwehr* (anti-aircraft, used for Army AA units)

Flak = *Flieger Abwehr Kanone* (anti-aircraft artillery)

Funk = radio

Gefechtstross = combat train

gem = *gemischte* (mixed)

Geo = *Geologen* (geological)

gepanzert = armoured

GFP = *Geheime Feldpolizei* (secret field police)

GK = *Gebirgs Kanone* (mountain gun)

HKAA = *Heeres Küsten Artillerie Abteilung* (army coastal artillery battalion)

IG = *Infanterie Geschütz* (infantry gun)

Inst = *Instandsetzung* (maintenance)

IR = *Infanterie Regiment* (infantry regiment)

K = *Kanone* (gun)

Kartenstelle = mapping detachment

KaSta = *Kampf Staffel* (combat detachment)

Kdr/Kdt = *Kommandeur/Kommandant* (commander)

Kfz = *Kraftfahrzeug* (vehicle)

KGr = *Kampfgruppe* (battle group)

Kol, K = *Kolonne* (column)

Korück = *Kommandant Rückwartige Armeegebiet* (commander of army rear areas)

Kp, Komp = *Kompanie* (company)

Krad = *Kradschützen* (motorcycle infantry)

Kraftwagen, Kw = motor vehicle

Krankenkraftwagen = ambulance

Kriegsgef = *Kriegsgefangen* (POW)

Kwk = *Kampfwagen Kanone* (tank gun)

Leichte, le, l = light

MG = *Maschinengewehr* (machine gun)

Mittlere = medium

mot = *motorisiert* (motorized)

MP = *Maschinen Pistole* (machine pistol)

Nachr = *Nachrichten* (communication)

Nachsch = *Nachschub* (supply)

Pak = *Panzer Abwehr Kanone* (anti-tank gun)

Pi, Pion = *Pionier* (engineer, sapper)

Prop = *Propaganda* (propaganda)

Pz = *Panzer* (tank, armour)

PzAOK = *Panzer Armeeoberkommando* (Panzer Army)

PzB = *Panzerbüchse* (anti-tank rifle)

PzGr = *Panzergruppe* (armoured group)

PzGr = *Panzergranate* (armour piercing shell)

PzGren = *Panzer Grenadier* (armoured infantry)

PzJäg = *Panzerjäger* (anti-tank)

PzKpfw = *Panzerkampfwagen* (tank, AFV)

OKH = Oberkommando des Heeres (Army High Command)

(r) = *russisch* (Russian)

Rgt = *Regiment* (regiment)

Sanitäts = medical

Schlachterei = butcher

Schtz = *Schützen* (light infantry)

Schwere, schw, s = heavy

SdKfz = *Sondern Kraftfahrzeug* (special vehicle)

SdVbd = *Sonder Verband* (special unit)

sfl = *Selbstfahrlafette* (self-propelled)

Späh = scout (used for AC units)

SPW = *Schützen Panzer Wagen* (armoured personnel carriers)

SR = *Schützen Regiment* (motorized infantry regiment)

St, Stab = HQ, staff

Stf, Staffel = squadron

(t) = *tschechisch* (Czech)

Trop = *Tropen* (tropical)

Trupp = section

Verm = *Vermessung* (survey)

Wach = security unit

Wasser = water

Werk = *Werkstatt* (workshop)

zbV = *zur besonderen Verwendung* (for special purposes)

Zug = platoon

Officers' rank conversion table

Leutnant = Lieutenant	**Generalleutnant** = Brigadier
Oberleutnant = First Lieutenant	**Generalmajor** = Lieutenant General
Hauptmann = Captain	**General der …** = Major General
Major = Major	**Generaloberst** = General
Oberstleutnant = Lieutenant Colonel	**Generalfeldmarschall** = Field Marshal
Oberst = Colonel	

Index

95